COMPLIMENTS OF UNISYS

LEADING SUPPLIER OF
OPEN SYSTEM SOLUTIONS
215-278-5530

D1532291

Crisis in Technology

CRISIS IN TECHNOLOGY

The Solution:
Strategic Weapons And Tactics
for Executives

**Handbook for Implementing
Strategic Advantage through
Technology**

JOHN J. DONOVAN

CAMBRIDGE TECHNOLOGY GROUP, INC.
CAMBRIDGE, MASSACHUSETTS 1990

AS/400 is a trademark of IBM.
CAMBRIDGE METHOD is a service mark of the Cambridge Technology Group, Inc.
DataHandler is a trademark of the Cambridge Technology Group, Inc.
Dataphone II is a trademark of AT&T.
DECnet is a trademark of Digital Equipment Corporation.
Lotus 1-2-3 is a trademark of Lotus Development Corporation.
MS-DOS is a trademark of Microsoft.
Netcon is a trademark of GDC.
NetDoc is a trademark of the Cambridge Technology Group, Inc.
Netman is a trademark of Uccel.
NetView is a trademark of IBM.
Supernet is a service mark of the Cambridge Technology Group, Inc.
SURROUND is a service mark of the Cambridge Technology Group, Inc.
Talkasync is a trademark of Cambridge Technology Group, Inc.
Talksna is a trademark of the Cambridge Technology Group, Inc.
UNIX is a trademark of AT&T.
VMS is a trademark of Digital Equipment Corporation.

Printing Number 885121
ISBN 0-9621794-0-X

Manufactured in the United States of America
Published February 1989, March 1989, March 1990
Third Printing

Acknowledgments

On January 18th, 1988, 9:00 A.M., the professional staff of the Cambridge Technology Group assembled to put down their actual experiences in using the tools and methodologies used at Cambridge to identify and implement our clients' most strategic needs. These people are the people who have worked with 47% of the Fortune 500, built 200 strategic applications and worked with over 800 other organizations. Their mission was to articulate and document that embodiment of knowledge and experience they had acquired.

These professionals included:

Maura Belliveau	Carl Giallombardo	Skip Rosenthal
Bruce Bigby	Holly Goodrich	Tina Sabin Sterpe
Michelle Blake	Drew Harman	Susan Senator
George Borhegyi	Tracy Harper	Allen Shaheen
Sarah Brubaker	Julie Heffernan	Stephen Shenefield
Don Bunker	Bill Hughes	Joe Shinn
Misa Burnett	Robert Jen	Meg Smyth
Linda Chow	Matthew Kaplan	Julianne Sprague
Theresa Chow	Maura Kelly	William Stanton
Joyce Chung	Jim Keydel	Mike Pavone
Susan Connolly	Hauke Kite–Powell	Kathy Stunkard
Maryellen Costello	Howard Kolodny	Tricia Sullivan
Sheeroy Desai	Michael Kolodny	Paul Tucceri

Maureen Donfield	Larry Krakauer	Todd Virtue
Pam Donnelly	Jim Markiewicz	Sherry Volk
Ryan Falvey	Theresa Markiewicz	Denise Weaver Ross
Dave Freedman	Carrie Murphy	Robin Whitworth
Doug Fulton	Alan Norquist	Cedric Williams
Valerie Germain	Betsy Olsen	Laura Zak
		Hope Zhang

These people are all authors of this book in the truest sense of the word. It is an honor for me and our customers to have worked with them.

In addition, we would all like to acknowledge all of our client organizations who have given us the privilege of working with them and the opportunity to put our methodologies into practice. Some organizations have developed very confidential applications not discussed here. Other cases appear here in generalized form so that you, too, may benefit. In both circumstances, we acknowledge these organizations' efforts and contributions.

I also wish to acknowledge my wife, Mary Jo, for both her intellectual contributions and for making the moments better for us all.

J.J.D.

Contents

/ CONTENTS

iv

/ CONTENTS

vi

Preface

Flash! For hundreds of years the Chinese used gunpowder for fireworks. They never implemented gunpowder as a strategic weapon until it was too late.

For many organizations, the ability to identify and apply the appropriate computing and communications options will largely determine how competitive they will be in the coming decade. We are already seeing organizations that face dissolution for the lack of an appropriate information system. Indeed, the questions raised about the role of computerized trading in the October 1987 stock market crash suggest that, to a large extent, the health of the entire world's economy is already tied to the workings of information systems.

As an executive, you are facing a highly competitive, turbulent environment that threatens the very survival of your organization and demands a confident and timely response to issues such as:

· **Opportunity**
  When mergers occur, there is an opportunity to take advantage of merging product lines, inventory, purchasing, financial analysis, and providing a unified presentation to customers.

However, the existing incompatible information systems are impediments.

· Raise Revenue — Cut Cost

One city government came to the Cambridge Technology Group ("CTG") with a $30 million deficit and with city employees who hadn't seen a pay increase in six years.

· Improve Quality

An organization with concerns about product quality has to record equipment faults in seven unconnected and incompatible systems.

In almost every situation, there is a way to bring information technology to bear on these concerns. This book describes the method each of these organizations employed to successfully avert disaster and indeed thrive in today's competitive environment. In fact, this method is also generally applicable to your opportunities.

WAIT! Do not close this book thinking we are talking about back-office computing. We are discussing the new era of STRATEGIC uses of technology. Just a few years ago, applying information technology to strategic issues was considered exotic and leading edge. But as computing and communications technology has evolved from "back room" systems to "board room" strategic applications, they have also changed from yesterday's tactical devices to today's most strategic weapons in the corporate arsenal.

Consider these statistics:

· Ten years ago, seven out of the top ten banks in the world were U.S. banks. Now, ten out of the top ten are Japanese.[1]

· The U.S. steel industry has lost substantial market share to the Japanese, who have neither the raw materials indigenous to their country nor the markets to dominate in this industry.

· Out of approximately 10 million cars sold in the U.S. this year, nearly half will be imported.[2]

· Our balance of payments to the Japanese alone is $62 billion, and $0.25 of your tax dollar now goes to paying the interest on the national debt.[3]

· In insurance, a major U.S. agency lost $72 million last year in just one division.

[1]*New York Times*, July 20, 1988.
[2]Lee Iacocca, *Talking Straight*, 1988.
[3]*Ibid.*

Lurking beneath these dramatic issues is a related but somewhat mundane-sounding question that is almost always overlooked by executives. That is, once an organization has identified an opportunity for a strategic information system, <u>how can the application be implemented within an appropriate time frame and without compromising the strategic nature of the application</u>?

A SWAT approach has to be developed!

Executives are asking and the unfortunate internal systems personnel want to respond, but traditional approaches do not provide the tools to respond to strategic systems. The traditional technology is geared to tactical, high performance, long development time, back room systems. Today, your organization must build strategic, board room, user-driven systems.

The Cambridge Technology Group has been conducting a survey of top executives' major concerns. In two years, we've collected responses from more than 2,500 visiting executives representing over 1,200 organizations — including 47% of the Fortune 500, major non-profits, and government agencies. The responses have been remarkably consistent. Regardless of title or industry, senior managers seem obsessed with two issues. The first is the question of how to <u>identify strategic opportunities for their organizations</u>. The second is how to <u>get it implemented fast</u> — while managing the change in their organizations—change that is running roughshod over familiar but increasingly ineffective ways of functioning.

This book addresses the CEO and senior management, presenting them with methods of fulfilling the basic business goals of the organization. <u>Executives must come to grips with the fact that the inability of traditional approaches to turn out effective strategic information systems, in the exceedingly short time frames critical to their success, threatens to throttle even the most promising opportunities</u>. Responsibility for this issue can no longer be delegated to lower levels of management. Senior managers must become directly involved in planning, implementing and managing those applications of information technology that address the core goals of the organization.

Enter the CAMBRIDGE METHOD^{SM}!

Surprisingly, the process of developing information–technology–based solutions to key organizational challenges need not be complex, painful or even technologically involved. By merging an appropriate business perspective with an easily grasped technological approach, executives can effectively focus their own insight and the organization's resources onto the task. All without destroying current technology investment.

The process described in this book, the CAMBRIDGE METHOD^{SM}, has been effective in transforming many organization's strategic concerns, via information technology, into strategic solutions–fast. As an aside, our employees used advanced desk-top publishing capabilities to produce this book, allowing us strategic control and distribution — fast.

FORMAT

This book is designed as an executive handbook for approaching strategic applications. It is intended to provide you, the CEO, CFO, CIO, VP Marketing, and all senior management, with ideas for strategic applications and methods for bringing them into reality. The contents and style of the book are for senior management, from executive summaries to a larger typesize than in abstract theoretical books. It is written for you.

Each chapter begins with a summary of its first major points and concludes with a "to do" list of specific first steps. So let's start from step one, with an informal and straightforward methodology for focusing in on the right targets for strategic information technology.

The approach described here will not only assist you and your organization, but will also address the broader issue of the improvement of this country's competitive position. As economic power goes, ideological power also goes... If the global economic winners are societies based on the rights of the state over the rights of the individual, then my efforts in this book and in my organization have been in vain.

Cambridge, Massachusetts   John J. Donovan
February 1989

Vision to Reality

No company is safe...There is no such thing as a "solid," or even substantial, lead over one's competitors. Too much is changing for anyone to be complacent. Moreover, the 'champ to chump' cycles are growing ever shorter.

> Tom Peters
> in *Thriving on Chaos*

We must find ways to make our information systems competitive weapons for achieving our vision.

> George Moody, President,
> Security Pacific Corporation

...A runaway [is] a system that's millions over budget, years behind schedule, and — if ever completed — less effective than promised. A recent Peat Marwick Mitchell & Co. survey of 600 of the accounting firm's largest clients highlighted the problem: Some 35% currently have major runaways.

> *Business Week*
> November 7, 1988

HOSTAGE CRISIS

It would seem that many organizations are being held hostage by their current information technologies — or are they actually facing substantial opportunities for competitive advantage? The list grows longer every day:

- *A hospital faces the threat of losing its accreditation because of its inability to reconcile its billing and its patient care files.*

- *A large jet engine parts manufacturer faces a possible shutdown if it cannot comply with FAA demands for rapid tracking of parts from assembly room floor to final customer.*

- *The <u>Boston Globe</u>, 15 November 1988: "More than 2400 blood products were released improperly over a six-month period, and 518 of them were made available before all testing for deadly diseases had been completed..."*

- *A major securities firm and a bank merge, but are unable to seize the strategic opportunity of presenting a single, unified cus-*

tomer interface because of incompatible computer systems.

- *A Regional Bell Operating Company is angering customers and facing regulatory action over an error rate as high as 23 percent in bills to long distance carriers.*

- *An insurance company is losing business due to its 15-day lag in processing automobile insurance applications.*

- *A large city government faces an ongoing revenue crisis due in part to millions of dollars in delinquent payments for municipal services.*

CRISIS OR OPPORTUNITY?

These seven organizations face very different challenges in six different industries. But they also have one important thing in common: all of them have been able to forge solutions through the use of strategic information technology.

When is an information system strategic? <u>It is strategic when it enables an organization to meet its highest goals</u> whether that be survival, slashing costs or boosting revenues — not by a tenth of a percent, but by ten, twenty percent or more; when it can pro-

3

vide a means for sprinting ahead of competition; when it can open the door to new and lucrative lines of business; when it can solve acute problems or dramatically enhance the success of an enterprise.

Few organizations, regardless of industry or degree of success, can afford to ignore strategic information technology (IT). Those that do will eventually find competitors using strategic IT to tighten the screws on them. When that happens, an organization must play a game of catch-up —and it will probably lose. That is because the competitive edge set by the first strategic application in an industry has historically proven difficult and costly to dissolve.

If it is strategic, then it is needed now. However, even the most innovative and determined senior managers face a formidable barrier: traditional technologies are not geared towards quickly producing information systems, strategic or otherwise.

Suppose a senior executive of a large organization were to come up with a strategic information system idea. The idea might, for example, involve gathering information on customers' orders and combining it with information on inventory to come up with projections for over- or understocking. Or perhaps the organization wants distributors to tie into product data and pricing databases and then en-

4

ter orders on-line. Or perhaps sales data from different divisions could be compared with econometric data from an outside research firm, leading to improved sales forecasting and the identification of new opportunities.

Whatever the idea is, it probably involves taking different types of information locked away in several computers inside and outside of the organization, processing it, and then presenting it in a new form that's readily accessible to the right people.

RUNAWAYS

How long will it take to implement the idea, and how much will it cost? Typical figures for a major strategic application are three to four years and five million dollars or more. Despite all of this, finished applications often deliver less than half of the originally envisioned capabilities — if indeed they are ever completed at all.

Runaway systems that are over budget and behind schedule are increasingly becoming the rule rather than the exception. And they can end up costing much more than just money. As reported in *Business Week*, November 7, 1988:

· For Allstate Insurance, a five year development effort turned into a project expected to span over a decade. Originally targeted in 1982 as

5

costing $8 million and having a completion date of 1987, the project is now estimated at $100 million with a completion date of 1993.

. Blue Cross & Blue Shield United of Wisconsin tried to maintain its customer base against inroads by popular HMOs by developing a $200 million computer system. It was fatally flawed and the company consequently lost 35,000 of its policyholders. The system distributed $60 million in overpayments and duplicate checks, and degraded customer services before the system was brought under control.

If an application idea is strategic, competitors will think of it, too. In most cases, only one organization achieves the full potential benefits of the application — <u>the one that builds it first</u>.

Even if an organization is the first to introduce a certain strategic application, if it took years to build, it will probably be out-of-date by the time it's installed. <u>Strategic opportunities are moving targets</u>. The strategic opportunities of today will most likely be completely irrelevant two years from now.

<u>MIS departments are not to blame for the time lag</u>. The lag simply reflects the limits of the technologies and methodologies with which MIS is equipped. The

frustrating thing is that the most important element of strategic applications—the data—generally already resides on various computers in and out of the organization. If these systems could be linked in a useful way, the strategic application would fall out readily. Unfortunately, MIS is not equipped with the necessary tools to meld different computer systems. They must build from scratch, and this inflates both budgets and timetables.

CLOSING THE GAP

Currently there is a painful gap between the need to build strategic systems quickly and the availability of appropriate technologies and methodologies for doing so. As more organizations appoint chief information officers (CIOs) to bring computers into corporate strategies, more organizations find themselves staring at growing MIS bills with precious little to show for it. That's why *Business Week, Fortune* and *The Wall Street Journal* alternate articles hailing the age of strategic information systems with articles lamenting the disappointing payoff of computerization.

To close the gap, organizations must recognize that strategic applications should not be approached in the same way as traditional applications.

Because these crucial, high-payoff systems must be completed in a timely fashion, special methodologies and tools are needed that differ greatly from those currently in use at most MIS departments.

Secondly, users, strategic planners, and non-technical managers must drive the application-building process to ensure that the results meet strategic needs, and that the system will be accepted and used.

Finally, organizations must closely examine the economic justifications for potential applications by means of business case analyses, and prioritize applications by their expected payoffs.

Only recently have such "Special Weapons and Tactics" emerged. Unfortunately, most organizations remain oblivious to these new techniques. However, a growing number of organizations have turned to the new approach, and have found that strategic applications can be built in two months, rather than two to five years. The resulting applications have had far more impact on their organizations than conventional applications would have —not only because they were built in a twentieth of the time, but also because they were designed and partly built by business managers rather than by technicians.

FREEING THE HOSTAGES

The seven organizations whose problems were listed at the start of this chapter used the new approach to develop strategic applications capable of helping them face their respective challenges. Here is a brief description of each of these applications:

The Hospital. Goal: Retain accreditation by reconciling billing and patient tracking capabilities. Solution: An information system that immediately provides a patient's history, current diagnosis, room number, attending physicians, treatment, insurance status and a running bill.

The Engine Parts Manufacturer. Goal: Track each part instantly, by serial number, from the factory to the final user. Solution: An information system that allows the engineers to enter part and serial numbers on-line as they construct each engine, thereby providing single-point tracking of each part's life cycle.

The Blood Supplier. Goal: Save lives by providing safe blood in a timely fashion. Solution: An information system that coordinates the inventory of blood between regional centers and tracks blood

9

from the donor to the recipient, helping to ensure that safe blood products reach recipients.

The Securities Firm. Goal: Provide complete financial services to customers. Solution: An information system that seamlessly integrates the two companies' systems to provide company personnel and customers with a single interface to both banking and investment services.

The Regional Bell Operating Company. Goal: Gain customer confidence and avoid penalties by reconciling errors in bills to long distance carriers. Solution: An information system that analyzes circuits and locates discrepancies that cause billing errors.

The Insurance Company. Goal: Retain share of auto insurance business by shortening the time it takes to approve an application. Solution: An information system that automatically retrieves driver data from state motor vehicle databases and compares it to information from company databases, reducing the approval cycle from 15 days to 1 day.

The City Government. Goal: Improve collection rates on delinquent payments. Solution: An information system that consolidates billing for property taxes, water, municipal court fees, and police charges.

FIVE BASIC STEPS

There are five basic steps to the CAMBRIDGE METHOD^{SM} process of achieving organizational goals through information technology:

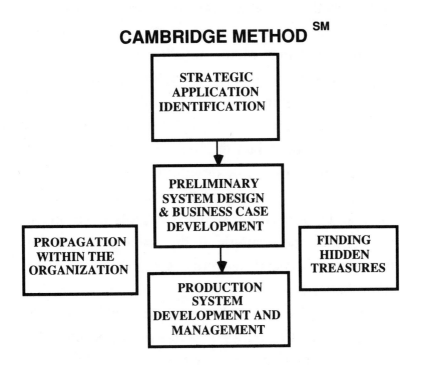

CAMBRIDGE METHOD ^{SM}

STRATEGIC
APPLICATION
IDENTIFICATION

PRELIMINARY
SYSTEM DESIGN
& BUSINESS CASE
DEVELOPMENT

PROPAGATION
WITHIN THE
ORGANIZATION

FINDING
HIDDEN
TREASURES

PRODUCTION
SYSTEM
DEVELOPMENT AND
MANAGEMENT

The challenge of the first step is to identify strategic applications which if deployed will have a major impact on corporate operations versus tactical applications of lower priority. This requires education of those entrusted with the strategic issues facing the company in a new approach, SURROUND^{SM}, which permits the rapid implementation of these applications without requiring a complete overhaul of existing information processing assets.

The challenge of the second step is to prove that the strategic application is feasible to implement, and to establish a sound business basis for proceeding. If your organization has ever been a victim of a runaway system implementation, this step is imperative. It will allow you to ferret out the strategic impact in cold financial terms and also force closure with the ultimate users of the application that their needs will indeed be met, before you make a major investment in full scale development.

The challenge of the production system development and management step is to rapidly develop and then deploy the strategic applications prototyped in the second step so the corporation can gain the maximum benefit.

Without the first and second steps, organizations would build information systems of minor impact or underestimate their cost of development. And without the production development and management step, even the most ingenious strategic application would end up sputtering and spinning its wheels trying to get off the deck.

In order to avoid the one shot syndrome, plans must also be established to propagate their new capability to the internal MIS staff so they become empowered to apply it on a corporate–wide basis. In addition, because the implementation of this method generates a new breed of innovative, strategic thinking through the organization, it is not unusual that corporations discover "hidden information treasures" which in their sales have enormous value. An example is customer or product information which using the CAMBRIDGE METHODˢᴹ and SURROUNDˢᴹ architecture becomes, for the first time, easily accessible and therefore marketable both within and perhaps outside the corporation.

FIRST STEPS

1. Do you want to be a winner or a loser? Are you willing to take the risks and pay the price to win? If you are, then read the rest of this book!

2. Begin by allocating the resources to form a dedicated SWAT team that will focus solely on strategic applications rather than tactical ones.

13

SUMMARY

- A strategic application must support an organization's critical success factors (CSFs), which in turn support the organization's goals. A goal is a fundamental end which an organization wants to achieve; a CSF is a *means* to that end.

- Be aware that not all applications are strategic to everyone — one organization's tactical application may be strategic to another organization.

- In many cases, threats may be turned into allies by assessing the strategic needs of an organization's customers and/or suppliers.

- Strategic applications often lead to the discovery of unexpected, albeit profitable, ways of capitalizing on or using the application. They can also lead to entirely new business opportunities.

Write down your organization's goals and supporting critical success factors, and have your colleagues do the same. Do you all agree on these? If

not, why not? Next, make a wish-list of strategic applications, ones from which your organization would benefit greatly. Finally, circle one that appears most critical.

What's Strategic and What Isn't

Every company has options open to it — sometimes they are numbered by the hundreds. Only a very few of these options constitute opportunities and only one or two of those are really strategic. The trick is to find that one or two.

V.P., Strategic Planning
A Regional Bell Operating Co.

Strategic or tactical?

...They'll march in to see me and announce that if we spend $25 million to put in this new mainframe from IBM, all of our systems will be able to talk to one another.

"Great," I tell them, " but what does that do for the company? How do we get more productive and build better products?"

"Glad you asked," they reply. "This mainframe is going to save us twenty-two new employees, easy."

So we invest in the computers and in training personnel — millions of dollars, thousands of hours — but we never go back and check on whether we saved ourselves even one person, let alone the twenty-two. I've signed so many projects that by now I should have nobody left. Yet I don't know that our decisions — or cars — get any better.

> Lee Iacocca
> in *Talking Straight*

"Solutions" to strategic problems are not found by detached analysts focusing coolly on the problem.

> Graham Allison
> in *Essence of Decision:*
> *Explaining the Cuban Missile Crisis.*

Ideas, like currency, tend to suffer from inflation. Take the idea of strategic information technology. When it first started popping up in academic circles in the early 1980s, the concept of strategic IT pointed the way to an entirely new direction for computerization. Traditional computer systems had been addressing mundane functions like accounting and clerical work — areas that may have benefited greatly from computerization, but that hardly accounted for more than a blip on annual reports. The new breed of strategic applications, on the other hand, was to be aimed at high-payoff, "mission-critical" functions. They would expand market shares, boost revenues, slash costs, and bring the organization into new lines of business. Their impact would be *dramatic*.

17

But the ravages of idea inflation have left us with a concept that is but a shadow of its former self. These days, the term "strategic application" is used to mean little more than "important application." And since organizations tend to consider all their computer applications important — why else would they be spending so many millions on MIS? — virtually any application fits the description. In some cases, the "strategic application" to which an executive refers is nothing more than a glorified accounting system (perhaps disguised as a "financial decision support system") or a word processing system (now blown up into "office automation").

Executives should take a good, hard look at their organization's projects. Are they really mission-critical? Are they projects that will make a significant difference to the success of the enterprise? Will they change the way the organization does business?

Relatively few organizations are working on information systems projects that can truly be considered strategic. Does this mean that other, non-strategic applications — e.g., payroll programs, which may not be strategic but are necessary — are a waste of time ? No — but by definition, only a fraction of an organization's worthwhile applications can be strategic.

The point is, that strategic fraction should be receiving a disproportionately large share of attention, in keeping with the disproportionately large payoff these applications promise. But when that fraction is zero, the organization has a problem—especially if its competitors have avoided falling into the same trap.

We're going to describe a simple technique for discovering ideas for strategic applications, eliminating the ideas that appear to be strategic but in fact miss the mark, and enhancing and refining winning ideas. But first, let's look at some case studies that illustrate basic categories of strategic applications.

APPLICATIONS THAT COULD SAVE AN ORGANIZATION

Whatever meaning gets attached to the term "strategic," most observers would probably agree that the term aptly applies to something that could conceivably mean the difference between an organization's survival and its potential failure. In many cases, an information system can help make that difference.

Textron Lycoming, a $7 billion conglomerate, was in need of such a critical application. As a manufacturer of gas turbine engines for commercial and military aircraft, Textron must be able to track every one of the millions of engine parts that it installs. Should a part later prove failure-prone, the company must be able to determine immediately what components of which engines in which vehicles belonging to what customers require attention. If it can't, the company might conceivably be shut down by the Federal Aviation Administration. Textron had been taking a risk by keeping track of parts through manually written logbooks, which made the task of quickly tracing parts nearly impossible.

What Textron needed —and in a hurry —was a way to automate the process of recording and tracking which parts went into which engines. With the stakes for part-tracking so high, no other system could have been considered more strategic. Textron recognized its need for such a system and built an application that allows engineers to enter part and serial numbers on-line as they construct the engine. The company can now instantly track down any part it has installed.

APPLICATIONS THAT COULD LEVERAGE AN ORGANIZATION

Some applications are capable of <u>lifting an organization out of a difficult and costly bind</u>. These just-plain-critical applications are also clearly strategic.

The Illinois Department of Employment Security pays out unemployment benefits and collects unemployment taxes. When the Department ran into problems a few years back collecting taxes from delinquent businesses, the federal government began making up the shortfall through interest-free loans. But then, when the Department's debt had already reached several billion dollars. The federal government imposed severe interest penalties. The Department was thrown into a serious cash–flow crisis. The only solution? To collect those revenues due from delinquent businesses of the state.

There were many thousands of delinquent businesses in the state. But given a limited number of collectors, it made sense to go after only those businesses that owed a relatively large sum of money and were capable of paying it. The problem was that manually gathering and analyzing the data necessary to identify these businesses would have taken all of the collectors' time in itself. To solve the problem, the Department built a system that could compare records located on several internal databases with information residing on outside financial databases. The system then turned out a list of potentially high-payoff, delinquent companies to target.

EVEN WELL-RUN ORGANIZATIONS CAN BENEFIT

In the above examples we looked at situations where applications helped avert a potential crisis. What about organizations that aren't facing serious crises—can their systems be considered strategic? <u>They can if the payoff is dramatic</u>.

The case of Eli Lilly provides an example of a non-critical, high-payoff system. The company was getting by with manually gathered clinical trial reports; but the opportunity to shorten the cycle offered such a huge reward — $7 for every second shaved off of each drug's testing cycle — that building an application to shorten the process had to be considered strategic.

Xerox's copier division also identified the need for a high-payoff application. The company was spending an average of $127 to process every one of its copier product orders — a cost that was nearly eliminating the profits from some low-end products, which were priced starting at $200. The high cost stemmed from the fact that orders were hand-written and then entered separately on four different types of systems: one for order entry, one for shipping, one for customer information, and one for billing. In addition, different types of products were handled by different order-entry systems.

As a result of this jigsaw puzzle of data, details of the order were being misrecorded or overlooked. A large copier might be delivered to a customer, for example, before arrangements had been made to install the required type of electrical outlet. When Xerox was forced to reprocess orders, customers might have been irritated by the resulting delays.

Simplifying order entry systems is always nice, but it isn't always strategic. When a revamped system promises to restore lost profits and soothe angry customers, however, it is nothing if not strategic. Xerox recognized this, and built an application that provided a unified picture of all information relating to an order, eliminating re-entering data and making it difficult to overlook important details. Not only did the application cut down turn-around time and errors, but, as a bonus, it slashed the costly training required by the complex multiple systems.

DECISIONS, DECISIONS

Another type of high-payoff application is one that provides information to help managers make decisions key to the success of the organization. Prudential Insurance decided it needed such a decision support system to improve its underwriters' ability

23

to set premiums on commercial insurance policies.

Setting premiums is a tricky business. If they're too low, then the claims the insurance company pays out are likely to exceed the income from its premiums. Prudential, in fact, was losing tens of millions a year to low premiums. But if underwriters re-rate premiums too high, the company inevitably loses business.

Prudential's underwriters had been making their decisions by digging up whatever data they could find on a customer's past premiums and claims, and then typing it into a Lotus 1-2-3 spreadsheet. This was an error-prone process that provided relatively little insight into whether a premium would prove sufficient. It also took up a lot of the underwriters' time, which cut the decision-making process too short and left them unavailable to handle the new insurance products Prudential wanted to introduce.

So Prudential built a system that automatically pulls down a wealth of current and historical premium and claim data, along with customer financial and credit information, from three different databases inside and outside of the company. This information is automatically loaded into Lotus 1-2-3. The underwriters now have more information to back up their decisions and more time to make them. The system even saves on clerical work: after the under-writers determine the premiums, the system auto-matically types out a letter to the customer detailing the figures.

WHEN INFORMATION IS STRATEGIC IN ITS OWN RIGHT

Occasionally, just having a certain type of infor-mation on hand can be strategic. A unique example is provided by the Church of Jesus Christ of the Latter-day Saints.

The Mormons, as they are popularly known, be-lieve that members can retroactively baptize and hence save long-gone ancestors. As long as genea-logical information on the ancestors is available, saving them becomes possible. Church doctrine states that the baptism has to take place before the Second Coming, so the Mormons feel they need to gather as much ancestral information as they can as quickly as possible.

The Mormons estimate there are some 7 billion documents around the world of genealogical signifi-cance to them; 2 billion of these are already on Church databases or microfiche. Speeding up the process of recording the remaining 5 billion or so documents is strategic to the Church. To that end, the Mormons built an application that makes it easy for

25

members to enter genealogical data on personal computers scattered throughout the country and then have the data automatically sent to a central Church database.

THE STRATEGIC MODEL

In reading cases such as the ones above, it often seems that the choice of strategic application was obvious. That's a misperception, however. Many, or even most, application ideas that at first seem strategic often fall short of having a significant impact on the elements of the business that really need it. The truly strategic ideas are often buried among these lesser proposals, and it takes a discerning eye to pull them out. It's only in hindsight that they seem obvious.

We use a simple model at the Cambridge Technology Group to help organizations identify the appropriate strategic targets for information systems. Here's the model: A STRATEGIC APPLICATION must support an organization's CRITICAL SUCCESS FACTORS, which in turn support the organization's GOALS.*

*The critical success factor concept was developed by Professor Jack Rockart of the Sloan School of Management. For further information, see John F. Rockart and David W. Delong, *Executive Support Systems*, Dow Jones-Irwin, 1988.

How do we distinguish a critical success factor (CSF) from a goal? <u>A goal is a fundamental end which an organization wants to achieve; a CSF is a *means* to that end.</u>

Take the example of Kodak's copier division. Kodak decided that customer satisfaction is its top goal. There are a number of things Kodak can do to help keep its customers happy — but not all of them would be critical. Building in product reliability and providing speedy service would both be critical success factors, for example, while offering the most sophisticated features wouldn't be. Customers like advanced features, of course; but they'd give them up without a second thought for a copier that never broke down. A fussy machine that takes days to service wouldn't last long on the market no matter how impressive its bells and whistles.

Exotic sports cars, on the other hand, are bought for style and performance. Aficionados are more than willing to put up with the finicky nature of these machines. For Ferrari, then, reliability would be important but not critical, while sophisticated design would be a full-fledged CSF.

There are no hard and fast rules as to what constitutes a CSF, just as there are no rules as to what constitutes an organization's goals. Both must be determined by top managers familiar with the or-

27

ganization's products, operations, customers and competitors. The point is, <u>managers have to hold off on picking a strategic application until they are certain they've accurately focused in on the truly critical success factors that contribute to key organizational goals</u>. Let's take a look at some examples of how the strategic model can help with this process.

ARE YOU SURE IT'S CRITICAL?

Von Duprin is a $50 million subsidiary of Ingersoll Rand that manufactures the push-bar mechanisms that unlatch exit doors in public locations. Though it has a 52 percent share of the lucrative market for these products, Von Duprin was concerned about an increase in customer complaints translating into a loss of business. The company's goal, then, was to boost customer satisfaction.

Since most of the complaints it received related to problems with order fulfillment, Von Duprin's executives figured that an enhanced order entry system would be strategic. The new system would be easier to use, so fewer mistakes and delays would occur.

There is no question that a new order entry system would have helped Von Duprin move closer to its goal of increased customer satisfaction. But before building the application, Von Duprin applied the strategic model to its situation, and realized that it hadn't thought out which elements of customer service were critical to its goal.

In talking to customers, the company discovered that there were two general complaints that seemed to be at the core of the problem. First, customers felt it was taking Von Duprin too long to fulfill orders — even when there were no errors in the ordering process. And second, customers perceived the customer sales and support phone operators to be unfriendly and unhelpful in answering questions about prices and order status. There were two critical success factor, then: cutting perceived order turn-around time, and making it more inviting for customers to get information on prices and order status. An enhanced order entry system wasn't likely to go a long way towards fulfilling these CSFs.

Von Duprin came up with a strategic application that would better address these CSFs. By tying customers directly into the company's order entry systems through an easy–to–use personal computer interface, customers could place orders themselves and cut out the several days often required to process a paper purchase order. The system would also allow customers to request pricing and order status information from the computer over a touch-tone phone, with responses delivered by a synthesized voice. In addition to speeding turn-around and eliminating customer irritation with operators, there would be a psychological benefit: dealing directly with Von Duprin's computer systems would give customers a greater sense of control over the ordering process, reducing frustration over delivery delays that might be unavoidable.

As another example, a major hotel chain set a goal of increasing its hotel revenues by seizing on the obvious success factor of boosting occupancy rates. On further reflection, however, the hotel chain decided that maximizing yield, and not occupancy rates, was critical to its goal. Yield takes into account not only the number of rooms that are filled, but also how much money the hotel is charging for each room it fills. The company then thought up a strategic system to help calculate the maximum rate it could charge for its rooms at a given time of year without significantly lowering occupancy rates.

TURNING COMPETITIVE FORCES INTO ALLIES

In many cases, following the strategic model should include an excursion into the strategic models of the external forces that affect your competitive position: your customers or suppliers, and maybe even *their* customers or suppliers. Identify the goals and CSFs of the organizations that are competitive forces, and examine ways in which your proposed application could enhance your relationship with these forces. Chances are good that you'll find ways to help these organizations reach their own goals by including them in the application you are designing. And if you can do that, you're well on the way to turning potentially harmful competitive forces into steady allies.

The basic idea is straightforward: by tying other elements of the customer and supplier "chain" into your application, you can give them access to valuable information and enhance the value of your system for everyone on the "chain," including yourself. That's what a major supplier of blood products did in designing its strategic blood services application.*

The supplier's goal is to save lives. Critical success factors include being able to provide needed blood quickly, and being able to quickly trace the source of any unit of blood when necessary. The

*For more information, see "The American Red Cross National Networking System," published in 1988 by the American Red Cross Blood Services, Northeast Region, 180 Rustcraft Road, Dedham, Massachusetts, 02026.

31

supplier designed an integrated inventory management system that fulfilled these CSFs. One key aspect of the application involved placing terminals in hospitals so that hospitals could order blood directly from the supplier's system. Clearly, the system's success would depend at least in part on whether or not hospitals would be willing to use the new terminals.

To devise a strategy for convincing hospitals to embrace the system, the supplier thought about the hospitals' (customers') goals and CSFs. Hospitals want to save lives and to reduce costs, and a CSF is to manage blood inventory effectively. As a result, the supplier added features to help hospitals save money by keeping blood supplies at appropriate levels.

Pursuing the chain further, we can find additional profitable linkages. Doctors are a critical resource for hospitals, and can even be considered "suppliers" of the hospitals since they are often the hospitals' main channel for patients. By placing terminals in doctors' offices, the hospitals can strengthen their link to the doctors by providing such services as online medical literature searches, direct access to insurance companies for faster claims processing, and direct access to the hospitals' patient records and registration. At the same time, the hospitals' blood inventory management systems could be improved by allowing doctors to schedule operations and associated blood requirements on-line, thereby further streamlining the blood ordering process and reducing the need for costly inventory holdings.

Information is valuable to almost everyone! Creative linkages to organizations that can affect your competitive position are well worth seeking out: they serve the double purpose of strengthening your ties to them and enhancing the value of your application.

LOOPING BACK

After successfully applying the strategic model and arriving at a winning application idea, it's worth going back through the model to discover ways of getting more benefits. Are there other CSFs that the system might be able to address? Are there entirely different goals whose CSFs can be supported through the same application?

Blue Cross/Blue Shield of Indiana wanted an application that would contribute to the goal of protecting its share of the health insurance market from the encroachment of health maintenance organizations. An associated critical success factor was improving its ability to respond to customer inquiries about claims. The company finally arrived at an application that would involve placing computer terminals in public places, allowing customers to walk up and retrieve information about policies and claims in much the same way they would use a bank's automated teller machine.

Then Blue Cross executives looped back through the strategic model and considered a second organizational goal: entering new insurance markets. One critical success factor was making it easy for customers to find out about and purchase Blue Cross's new life insurance products. The executives realized the same application could be extended to support this new CSF. The public terminals could encourage customers to retrieve information on life insurance prices and benefits, and could even sell the insurance on the spot.

TURNING THE MODEL AROUND

There's more mileage to be squeezed out of the model: <u>by turning the process around, the application can lead to new business strategies — and even new lines of business — that hadn't occurred to managers before</u>.

The most obvious way to establish a new business opportunity based on a strategic application is to sell the system to non-competitive organizations with similar critical success factors. That's what Pacific Northwest Bell* did by offering its strategic application — circuit data reconciliation — to other telephone companies.

But many organizations find they are able to devise entirely unique strategies based on their applications. Such unexpected opportunities can be the most exciting aspect of planning a strategic application.

A region of the American Automobile Association was looking for an application that would further its goal of improved member satisfaction. Its critical success factor: speed up the time it takes to get a tow truck to a member's disabled vehicle. When a member in need of towing or repair services called AAA's national 800 number, an operator would take down the caller's location and membership number. After hanging up, or while the member waited on hold, the operator would access a central database of membership information to verify the validity of the membership number. Then the operator would access one of several regional databases listing participating service stations to determine

*For further information, see "DRIVER: Reliable Database Verification," published in 1987 by Pacific Northwest Bell, 1600-7th Ave. Seattle, WA 98191.

which was closest to the disabled car. Only after this time-consuming process would a call go out to the service station.

The regions decided it needed a system that would let an operator simply type in the caller's membership and location. The system would then automatically and simultaneously access the membership database and the appropriate regional service station database, verify the membership number and return the phone number of the nearest service station in seconds. That could cut minutes off the time required for an operator to do it manually—and off the time a member might have to stand in the cold waiting for the tow truck.

The application definitely addressed the CSF. But before stopping there, the region's AAA executives asked themselves if there might be some other use for their new-found access to information. The new system could easily track which members broke down and where. But for whom would this timely list of recent breakdowns constitute a CSF?

From the fact that a large percentage of the calls to AAA are from members with flat tires, combined with the knowledge that most people buy new tires within a few days of getting a flat, the executives realized that local tire dealers might be extremely interested in an up-to-the-minute list of people who had suffered flats in their area. Aided by such a list, a dealer could place a quick call or send out a flyer to these people to plug its special of the week. Since thousands of tire dealers across the country might be willing to pay for this type of information, the region's AAA managers felt they had uncovered a potentially lucrative new source of revenue—and they did it by working backwards from their original application idea.

WINDFALL PAYOFF

In another case, the Elizabethtown (New Jersey) Gas Company had been tracking its complex network of pipes primarily through hand-drawn maps and file cards. As a result, keeping track of pipes for maintenance, emergencies and new construction was a difficult chore. But when it took over an hour to locate a leaking pipe's shut-off valves after a house in its service area exploded, the company decided it needed an application that would provide instant access to pipe and valve locations.

The application would satisfy the critical success factor of locating active pipes quickly. But in experimenting with the system, company executives found it was also possible to point out a large network of older, abandoned pipes unsuitable for carrying gas. In thinking about it, executives realized that local ca-

37

ble TV companies could save hundreds of thousands of dollars in conduit-laying costs by running cables through these abandoned pipes. Presumably, the cable companies would be willing to pay for such an opportunity. Again, potentially, an entirely new source of revenue had been sifted out of a strategic application.

The fact that such examples address unusual circumstances may cause managers to question whether their organization is likely to achieve a similar unexpected reward from a strategic application. Actually, <u>we've found that such seemingly "windfall" payoffs are more the rule than the exception. Most organizations face a virtually limitless number of business opportunities; taking advantage of these opportunities requires only imagination and the right opening. A strategic application often provides the opening.</u> The strategic model can help point the way.

VISION TO REALITY: IMPLEMENTATION

Now it's time to shift our focus to an entirely new set of concerns: how applications get beyond the idea stage. That's what we'll tackle in the next chapters. First, we'll examine a radically new approach to implementing your strategic systems — an approach that will cut the time-frame and project costs by an order of magnitude or more over traditional approaches.

FIRST STEPS

1. Establish the goals and critical success factors (CSFs) of your organization with your colleagues. These aren't set in stone — an organization's goals and CSFs can, and should, be re-evaluated and modified over time.
2. Identify the external forces affecting your organization's competitive position (e.g., customers, legislators, suppliers...).
3. Identify the goals and CSFs of each of these entities that represent these external forces.
4. Identify ways in which your organization can help these organizations (forces) to attain their goals (particularly through the use of information), thereby turning these forces into allies.

SUMMARY

In implementing *strategic applications*, three factors must be addressed:

1. **Time**: you need it immediately. Traditional approaches take too long.

2. **User involvement**: the user must drive the process. Traditional approaches typically have the technical people driving the process.

3. **Adaptability to changes**: changes in *use, technology,* and *need* will occur and must be incorporated immediately.

The CAMBRIDGE METHOD^{SM} and the SURROUND^{SM} architecture does it all!

The Magic Of The SURROUND^{SM} Strategy

The Magic

Amazing stuff! And this is not stuff that we are going to have to try to <u>sell</u> to our clients, this is stuff that our clients are telling us <u>they</u> want!

> Deborah Kowalczyk, Asst. V.P
> CIGNA Investment Group

After building the SURROUND^{SM} system, we are cocky! All we have to do is identify the most strategic opportunities, and then we can <u>do</u> it. And that's the bottom line.

> Steve Masie, Design Supervisor
> Manufacturing Systems
> Textron Lycoming

Rapid Development

What you see here will shrink our time frames when we look at developing the systems that we need to be competitive.

> George Varga, V.P.,
> CIGNA Investment Group

41

User Involvement

I'm a user, but I built those screens — I'm going to use them!

> Paul Dunay, Manager,
> Textron Lycoming

Transition to Pillage & Burn

The SURROUND^{SM} technology will allow us to protect the investments in our core systems, while reducing the time frame to implement the strategic systems for our corporation.

> John Singleton
> Vice Chairman of the Board
> Security Pacific Corporation

Connectivity

Connectivity of diverse systems is extremely important. Due to the government's contracting policies, we have many different types of systems. We must make them work together since we can never specify manufacturers.

> Lt. Colonel John Heitman
> United States Air Force
> Standard Systems Center

Change in Technology

The most dramatic improvements in computing in the next five years will be in user interfaces.

> Professor Nicolas Negroponte
> Director, Media Lab
> Professor of Media Technology
> MIT

You have identified a strategic information technology application. Now it's time to implement it. But unless the application is unusually simple, the developers will ask for a budget in the millions or even tens of millions and will want years to complete it. Consultants will most likely say the same. Computer manufacturers will agree and suggest that additional computers are needed as well. Software vendors will push state–of–the–art application development tools, promising these tools will cut development time from three years to a year–and–a–half, but only after your technical people have gone through the ordeal of extensive retraining.

<u>That's why everyone talks about strategic technology and no one does anything about it</u>.

This year, the management of a major U.S. bank set out to increase the bank's market share of the metropolitan area from 9 percent to 20 percent over a nine month period. To that end, management identified two critical success factors: acquiring competitive banks and increasing customer satisfaction. The second factor seemed to fall out naturally from the first, since customers could reasonably be expected to like having access to a greater number of branches.

Then the bank's technical resources dropped a bombshell: it could take years to integrate the bank's computer systems with those of its acquisitions. Until then, a bank customer walking into a newly acquired branch to cash a check would have to be turned away; the teller wouldn't be able to access that customer's account information. If the bank couldn't find a way to integrate the systems quickly, its acquisition strategy might actually hurt customer satisfaction. Information technology had suddenly become highly strategic.

PILLAGE AND BURN

When faced with dramatically new information systems needs, most organizations end up taking a "pillage and burn" approach — that is, they more or less scrap their old systems and build a new one from scratch. Why take this drastic approach? Because we *supposedly* know that the complex series of programs that make up the software component of a large system can't be radically altered in any practical way, nor can different systems be intimately linked when the need arises. That's *supposedly* true when the different systems have been designed to run on computers from different manufacturers. In fact, one of our example bank's first acquisitions has Burroughs computers while its new parent's systems are designed for IBM computers.

The obvious solution has traditionally been to pillage and burn. The approach has some advantages. The new system design can be tailored to the exact needs of the organization (or at least to the needs as they exist during the design stage). In addition, a single new system can replace a number of older, incompatible systems, as was the goal of our bank.

PILLAGE AND BURN: THE SINGE

But there are distinct drawbacks to the pillage and burn approach. For one thing, an organization's information systems needs change, typically between the time a system is designed and the time it's completed. <u>Brand new systems are often obsolete from day one</u>. This almost certainly would have been the case for our bank; even as a new system was being built, the parent company would be busy planning new banking products, not to mention acquiring more banks. If there were no good way to integrate these new banks and products into the new system, the corporation would end up right where it started.

PILLAGE AND BURN: TIME AND MONEY — RUNAWAY

Another factor is the time and money involved in building a new system. Our bank was told by one major computer company that a new system would cost tens of millions of dollars and take two years to complete. Tens of millions of dollars and two years before a customer could cash a check in an acquired branch! And these figures weren't excessive.

PILLAGE AND BURN: EXISTING CONSTRAINTS

For example, Xerox estimates it has $10 billion worth of existing data processing systems. <u>Clearly, its management would have to think twice before scrapping them for a new system, no matter how pressing the need</u>.

Simply stated, <u>the pillage and burn approach is wasteful.</u> After all, it's not that existing systems don't work; they often only require some crucial enhancement. Our bank's systems — along with those of its acquisitions — were all doing their jobs well. Their only shortcoming was that they couldn't share information and lacked some functionality. It seemed as if that would be enough, however, to force the bank to start all over again.

INFILTRATE

The MIS department might suggest an alternative: tellers could be given new, more flexible terminals capable of connecting to each bank's system separately. When a customer came in to cash a check, the teller could tie into the appropriate system — assuming the customer knew which bank kept his or her account information — to clear the transaction. But if the customer didn't remember where he or she first opened an account, the teller would have to keep searching through the different systems until the information was located, while customer lines backed into the street. This approach would also require retraining all tellers to use each of the different systems, a costly task that would take months; customer complaints would almost certainly pile up in the meantime. For these reasons, this *infiltrate* approach was deemed unacceptable.

The corporation's management was nearly resigned to the huge waste in time and money that building an entirely new system would entail. But at the last minute they decided to take a very different approach to solving their problem — an approach that would tie together all of their existing and acquired systems in a few months, and ensure that future acquisitions could be integrated within days.

The bank applied the SURROUND^{SM} architecture to its systems.

THE SIMPLICITY OF THE SURROUND^{SM} APPROACH

The SURROUND^{SM} architecture involves "hiding" existing computer systems behind a new, much more flexible, and more functional system. When employees sit down to use the new strategic application they interact only with this new SURROUND^{SM} system; the SURROUND^{SM} system then interacts with the older systems to get the information that the user needs.

Sample SURROUND ^{SM} Architecture

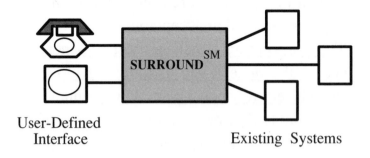

User-Defined
Interface

Existing Systems

The SURROUND^{SM} architecture includes three components:

- · Your existing systems and applications.
- · User interface devices and user–defined application.
- · Computer(s) which run the SURROUND^{SM} software to create a new strategic application by:
    1. Connecting to your existing systems
    2. Processing and storing information
    3. Interacting with the desired user interfaces

As will be discussed in Chapter 5, this computer can be *any vendor's* computer, provided that it has the appropriate connectivity, network management, and interface tools. Throughout this chapter, the shaded areas in the diagrams represent this software running on the SURROUND^{SM} computer.

THE SURROUND^{SM} APPROACH APPLIED

The SURROUND^{SM} system provides all the functionality required by the strategic application, such as integrating data from different systems and making the system easy to use. *The older systems need not be altered in any way*. The SURROUND^{SM} system can be built quickly and inexpensively because it uses a generic, "prefabricated" construction which doesn't require rebuilding the older systems' databases of information —the most time-consuming part of building a new application. <u>In most cases, a SURROUND^{SM}-based strategic application can be designed, built and installed in months</u>.

By the time our bank turned to the SURROUND^{SM} approach, it had already acquired a bank in its own state. This new bank's account information resides on a Burroughs computer within the state, while the parent bank's own account information is spread across three IBM computers in another state. The SURROUND^{SM}-based strategic application they built enables tellers in either bank to type any account number into their terminals. The SURROUND^{SM} system takes the account number, searches through all four systems in seconds, and provides the tellers with the appropriate account information.

New acquisitions can be quickly plugged into the same SURROUND^{SM} system. To the tellers, it looks as if they are interacting with a single database of account numbers, and the system is actually easier to use than their original, single-bank systems. This is because the flexibility of the SURROUND^{SM} approach can be turned <u>outwards</u> as well, to create user-de-

50

fined (and thus, by definition, user-friendly) interfaces.

CAN THE SURROUND^{SM} APPROACH GIVE THE "LITTLE GUY" AN ADVANTAGE?

The SURROUND^{SM} architecture can be applied to almost any strategic application. Take, for example, Covenant Insurance. Covenant wanted to speed the time it took to get auto insurance policy quotes back to its agents. The information it needed to process an application included premium and loss information, stored on an IBM computer; policy quote and numbering information, stored on a Wang computer; driver information, kept on computers at the state's department of motor vehicles; and financial business information from Dun and Bradstreet's computers.

Covenant hadn't been able to tie together these four systems (two of which were owned by other organizations, and thus couldn't be altered). By using the SURROUND^{SM} approach, however, Covenant was able to quickly build a system that retrieves the required information from all four systems. All a Covenant employee has to do is type in the appropriate policy and driver's license numbers, and the reports come back in seconds. The system is easy to use and enables underwriters to make yes or no decisions on the spot. The policy application processing time has thus been cut from 15 days to one day.

WHY HAVEN'T I HEARD OF THIS?

It all sounds simple enough, but this type of systems integration is virtually unheard of in the computer industry—and it is absolutely crucial to the ability to bring strategic applications on-line within reasonable time and budgetary constraints.

Some factors which have led to the mess which holds you hostage include: the <u>self-interest of vendors</u> in attempts to maintain profit margins on proprietary systems, a <u>comfort level</u> within MIS departments for "traditions" and antiquated "ways we do things around here," and the <u>lack of an absolute screaming demand</u> by users for the systems *they* want!

THE VERSATILITY OF THE SURROUND^{SM} APPROACH

There are several major areas of applicability of the SURROUND^{SM} approach. To provide you with a feeling for where SURROUND^{SM} can really pay off for you and your organization, let's talk about six major areas of applicability: rapid systems development, transitions to pillage and burn, connectivity, introducing new technologies, evolution to a gateway architecture, and starting from scratch. We'll also include an example where SURROUND^{SM} might be one solution, but not necessarily the *best* one.

RAPID SYSTEMS DEVELOPMENT: WHEN SPEED IS EVERYTHING

Some of the things that can be accomplished through the SURROUND^{SM} approach to systems development could also be accomplished through more traditional approaches; it would just take longer and cost more, by factors of tens, or even hundreds. <u>The time factor alone can make the difference between being in or out of business</u>.

Speed was crucial to a major hospital when it was notified by the State Board of Health that the hospital's difficulties in billing and in documenting patient care might cost it its accreditation. The hospital's ability to quickly build a patient information and billing system wasn't merely strategic; it was absolutely critical to the organization's survival.

In fact, the hospital already had all the information it needed, such as tracking of diagnoses, patient-physician pairings and room assignments, on its computers. <u>The problem was that the hospital had no way of getting these computers to work together to provide effective billing and patient care systems</u>. SURROUND^{SM} technology provided the required inte-

gration without duplicating the effort that was en-
capsulated in the existing system. We've got to
remember: if it's *strategic*, we need it **now**!

Rapid Development

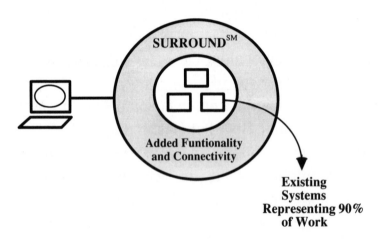

FOR TRANSITION TO PILLAGE AND BURN: BRIDGE OVER TROUBLED SYSTEMS

The SURROUND^{SM} approach doesn't preclude an organization from later deciding to pillage and burn its existing systems. In fact, <u>the SURROUND^{SM} approach can provide a crucial bridge between the old and new environments, providing immediate and continuous access to the new strategic capabilities while the organization gradually replaces its existing systems one at a time.</u>

When a major international courier service decided to replace its multiple billing systems with a new, integrated worldwide billing system, it assumed it would have to suffer with the old systems during the multi-year project development phase. Then the courier discovered that a SURROUND^{SM} version of the new system—a version which actually retrieves the data out of the old systems—can be brought up in just a few months. As the long-term version of the new system is built, it can be installed in pieces without interrupting the functioning of the SURROUND^{SM} environment. In addition, the courier has the option of building a new system by either allowing the SURROUND^{SM} environment to "close in" on the old systems—that is, simply to replace the old systems with an expanded version of the SUR-

55

ROUND^{SM} environment—or by building an entirely new environment that would eventually replace the SURROUND^{SM} system.

Transition to Pillage and Burn

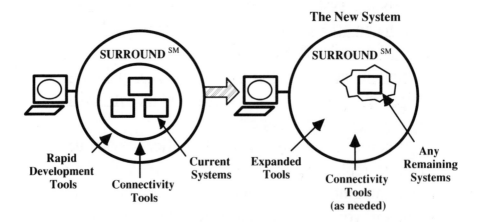

FOR CONNECTIVITY

Case: Connecting to PCs.

Most organizations are increasingly relying on personal computers to handle information applications. It's no wonder: PCs are cheaper to operate, easier to use, and provide individuals with greater control over their computer-dependent work. The only problem is that PC applications are often limited unless they have access to information that can't be stored on the PC itself. Some PC users need to plug in to databases stored on giant corporate mainframe systems, for example, while others need access to databases kept outside the organization.

The Church of Latter Day Saints encountered this problem. As mentioned in Chapter Two, one of the Mormons' critical success factors is to build a database of genealogical information for all its members. This enormous and rapidly growing database is stored on a large mainframe in "batch" fashion — that is, the information stored in the database can only be accessed and updated through an intermittent, time-consuming programming process. But genealogical information tends to turn up in small pieces that can't be handled effectively by this process. So the Mormons turned to PCs, which provide an easy-to-use, readily available vehicle for entering small pieces of data. But how could they get the data from the PCs onto their mainframe batch system? Though many software vendors promote their "PC–to–mainframe links," such links are highly restricted in their applications, and couldn't handle the Mormons' task.

Using SURROUND^{SM} technology, the Mormons were able to tie their PCs into the mainframe database. Because the batch mainframe is surrounded, and thus hidden from the PCs, the PC users continue to operate their application in exactly the same fashion, as if nothing has changed. Not only is the tie-in "transparent" to the PC users, but it is also invisible to the unaltered mainframe system, to which data was being uploaded automatically from the PCs. Any other approach would have required scrapping or changing the batch system — a daunting, and expensive, proposition.

Connectivity for Value-Added

We've seen that SURROUND^{SM} technology is capable of pulling in and integrating information from one or two systems that lie outside the organization. But some organizations formulate strategic application ideas that require tying into tens, or even hundreds, of outside computers representing a range of hardware and software environments. That can't be accomplished through conventional approaches, but it can with the SURROUND^{SM} approach.

Consider the situation of a state Department of Health, which wanted to collect patient information from nearly 300 independent hospitals scattered around the state. One technique would have been to apply the SURROUND^{SM} architecture to the Health Department's IBM mainframe. But even SUR-ROUND^{SM} technology might have faltered given the task of incorporating 300 different interfaces into a single system. So the Department tried it the other way around: each outside system can be provided with its own small-scale SURROUND^{SM} environment which hides the incompatibilities of the different systems. To the Department's mainframe, it looks as if it is dealing with 300 identical, fully compatible systems.

One problem remained: how could so many independent hospitals be convinced to apply the SURROUND^{SM} approach to their systems? The SURROUND^{SM} system doesn't interfere with the normal functioning of their systems, but MIS managers are typically wary of any alteration or addition to their environments. Then, of course, there is the cost of the SURROUND^{SM} systems—about $30,000 per hospital—which the Health Department wanted the individual hospitals to absorb. Providing the Department with information wasn't much of an incentive for the hospitals. The solution: build additional incentives into the SURROUND^{SM} environment.

Every hospital has to send information to a variety of public and private insurance institutions, as well as to research groups such as the National Cancer Registry. Since these varied reporting requirements bury hospitals in a costly mountain of paperwork, the Health Department guessed that hospitals would welcome the chance to have patient information automatically taken from their individual computers and shipped electronically—or via computer-printed letter—in the formats required by each organization.

In addition, the local SURROUND^{SM} environments can link the hospitals' registration, medical and billing systems to improve patient care and cash flow. Meanwhile, the SURROUND^{SM} systems can be sending the Health Department the information it needs. The Department has already successfully tested the approach with one medical center.

THE SURROUND^{SM} APPROACH FOR INTRODUCING NEW TECHNOLOGIES

Case: New Interface Technologies

In many cases, an organization's existing system works beautifully but is so complicated to use that extensive training is required for new users. Training is out of the question in some strategic applications, such as those where customers are expected to use the system. Would customers be happy with their banks' automated teller machines if they had to take a week-long training course on how to use them?

A large U.S. telecommunications operating company faced this issue when it decided that providing customers with speedier access to billing information would help achieve its goal of raising customer satisfaction. As it stood then, customers who wanted to check their billing status had to call a service representative, who then accessed the account information through a computer. There was often a wait to reach a service representative, so the operating company decided to let customers access the information directly from the computer, by dialing in and using the touch-tone keys of their phone to enter their account numbers; instructions and responses would be issued by a computer-synthesized voice.

Touch-tone information entry and synthesized voices are easily acquired technologies. <u>The problem for the operating company was how to add these "interface" technologies to its existing system, which was designed for use with a complicated, computer–terminal–oriented interface</u>. Normally, the existing system would have to be at least partly rebuilt. But using the SURROUND^{SM} approach, the company was able to separate its existing system from the interface. The existing system interacts with the SURROUND^{SM} environment, which "pretends" to be the same computer terminals the system was used to seeing. The touch-tone and synthesized voice interfaces are now attached to the SUR-

ROUND^{SM} environment which acts as an interpreter. In addition, now that the system is utilizing the SUR-ROUND^{SM} architecture, the company can add on any assortment of interfaces that suit its needs at a given time.

New Interface Technologies

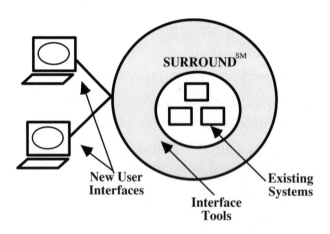

Case: New Processing Technologies.

Executives have been reading a great deal about the promise of new technologies such as expert systems, which allow computers to mimic human reasoning processes, and parallel processors, which deliver tremendous computing horsepower at low cost. MIS departments might in rare instances build new, isolated applications based on these technologies, but they lack a consistent means to tie them into existing systems. *Fortune* quoted one DuPont executive who was expecting a 1500 percent return on investment from an expert system—but noted that such returns depend on finding a way to hook these systems into corporate mainframe databases. In fact, there is a way to tie expert systems, or almost any new technology, into existing systems: the SURROUND^{SM} approach.

To another telecommunications operating company, incorporating expert systems into existing applications was crucial to its goals of increasing market share and raising customer satisfaction. The company knew how to use an expert system to analyze existing and proposed communications networks, but it was at a loss as to how to draw on its store of network specifications and other data that the expert system needed for the analysis. That information is dispersed across six different systems running on computers in several different states.

Working with the SURROUND^{SM} approach, the company was able to link the scattered systems. The SURROUND^{SM} environment automatically extracts the necessary information from each system and ships it to the expert system, running on a personal computer.

The same approach can be used to attach parallel processors, voice recognition systems, Reduced Instruction Set Computers (RISC), or other emerging technologies which may promise to revolutionize information technology. One of the great advantages of the SURROUND^{SM} approach to strategic information systems is that it allows an organization to virtually incorporate any type of existing or emerging computer technology into an organization's computing environment. <u>Organizations that look for opportunities to apply some of these new technologies stand to gain important competitive weapons; those that remain sleepily content with established applications will be the victims of these weapons.</u>

New Processing Technologies

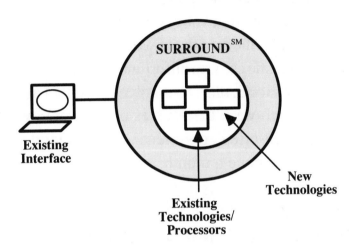

THE SURROUND℠ APPROACH FOR EVOLVING TO A GATEWAY ARCHITECTURE

The advent of high-powered, special-purpose database machines has made possible the ability to route data through a single machine whose dedicated purpose is the management of data. This machine, along with a SURROUND℠ computer, can serve as a "data gateway," allowing data to be routed from any application or system to any other application, system, or user interface.

The chairman of the board of one of the nation's top ten banks had a problem: he had no way of knowing, on any given day, how much money was in his bank, nor where that money might have come from. At the end of the month, he would have the answers to his questions, but unfortunately, the data was by then one month old. The problem was that all the systems which were the sources of his monthly report were batch-oriented systems, whose reports could only be run once a month.

Evolution To Gateway Architecture

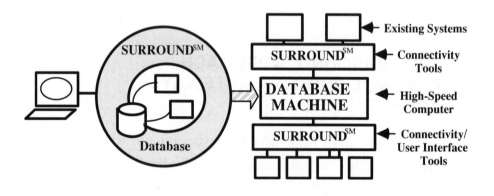

The solution to this problem is a transition to an on-line system, with a huge data warehouse (e.g. a database machine, such as Teradata) and on-line access. But this process will take some time — time that U.S. banks don't have! The SURROUND^{SM} architecture enables the feeding of data into an on-line database *in parallel* with the information flow to the current batch systems, thus allowing the existing systems to do their job while the new architecture can be used for on-line access to that data.

STARTING FROM SCRATCH: WHEN YOU'VE GOT TO BUILD THE CORE SYSTEMS

In cases where it has been concluded that a new system is in order, the SURROUND^{SM} methodology offers a modular, flexible, and easy approach to building systems. The ability of the SUR-ROUND^{SM} architecture to attach to many systems also applies when talking about sub-systems within a single project. This means that you can build your package in pieces, and see each of those parts running, *long before* the final system is completed.

A major U.S. organization needed to build a regional and national ordering and inventory system. They first built the 20 regional systems, and then independently surrounded these to produce the national system. After the core systems had been built, the SURROUND^{SM} architecture was again used to add specialized customer interfaces, as well as interfaces for management.

WHEN THE SURROUND^{SM} APPROACH ISN'T RIGHT

The SURROUND^{SM} approach offers tremendous advantages over any other approach when a strategic application requires changing, adding to, or linking existing systems. The majority of strategic applications falls in this category. But once in a while a strategic application will make information demands where <u>no systems exist or where the existing systems are not applicable</u>. In that situation, there is little else to do but pillage and burn.

The previously discussed hotel chain, (mentioned in Chapter 2) in keeping with their goal of increasing revenues, had identified as a critical success factor maximizing the "yield" of each room — that is, the price the hotel is able to charge, given availability and demand. To accomplish this, management envisioned a computer system that could review a hotel's historical occupancy rates, compare them to current bookings, and then determine the maximum yield on a daily or even hourly basis.

But such a system would need access to historical reservation and room rate information—information that the chain's inadequate systems simply couldn't provide on a consistent basis. In fact, in the entire country only two hotels had such hotel property management computers. The inevitable conclusion was to build these basic systems from scratch. Applying the SURROUND^{SM} architecture to the inadequate (or non-existing) systems couldn't have solved the information gap.

Such situations are the exception. In the great majority of cases, most of the information needed for a strategic application resides on a computer somewhere, just waiting to be turned to the organization's advantage — in other words, just waiting for the SURROUND^{SM} architecture.

FIRST STEPS:

1. Seek out your present *strategic opportunities*. Do not be unwilling to dream. Rank these ideas in order of their pay-off to you and your organization.

2. Identify an individual or several individuals who can dedicate themselves to making your vision a reality. Provide them with the proper training and tools to execute your opportunity.

3. The individuals you select should be given the support they require, but should feel the *urgency* of

your opportunity. For technical individuals, expose them intensively to the business aspects of your organization; for the business-oriented, give them a crash course in the technology.

IV

SUMMARY

- The real advocacy of a strategic system must rest with the burning passion of the visionaries within your organization.

- To supplement the passion and to gain broad-based support within the organization, financial benefits of strategic applications should be quantified in a business case.

- This analysis should take a minimum of time and effort, and should be based on the best conservative estimates provided by users of the system.

Take the strategic applications you identified in Chapter 2 and quantify the benefits of implementing the systems using either transaction or yearly cost savings or benefits. Estimate the cost of implementation using traditional approaches, and using the SURROUND^{SM} approach, within a framework of either transaction or yearly cost savings or benefits.

IV

The Litmus Test – $

Without a compelling business case, there is no point in proceeding.
> John Singleton, V. Chairman
> Security Pacific Corporation

Some of these savings appear to be so enormous that they jump off the page!
> Harry Hertrich
> Chief Financial Officer
> Lutheran Medical Center

If I/S is truly strategic, that is, capable of bringing about major changes in the organization—and of putting it at major risk—then it should be possible to estimate in advance what the costs and benefits of these changes will be. Failure to do so suggests...either bad strategy or bad analysis. In the new era of information systems, we can afford neither.
> Michael Vitale, V.P., I/S
> Prudential Insurance Company
> in *Information WEEK*, May 9, 1988

The Goals/Critical Success Factors model discussed in Chapter 2 helps determine when an application of information technology is truly strategic. But is that enough to justify undertaking the project? Many managers would feel it is—especially those assertive and expressive managers who tend to make decisions based on a qualitative, intuitive grasp of a situation.

Most managers, however, aren't comfortable making decisions without a hard-nosed analysis of the economics. Goals, critical success factors and strategic benefits won't totally address their idea of the bottom line. For these managers, the litmus test of a strategic application is a cost-benefit worksheet that answers one key question: What is the payoff? Step 2 of the CAMBRIDGE METHOD℠ answers this question.

DO THESE ACCOUNTING METHODS APPLY TO ALL SYSTEMS?

Much controversy exists over the methods employed and the validity of the results of measuring the financial benefits of information technology. The distinction we wish to make here is that these controversial approaches often have been applied to *tactical* systems. Our experience has shown that for strategic systems, the straight-forward method presented here provides the needed structure and supporting case for those in the organization that are concerned about quantifying costs and benefits. However, the real case for going forth with a strategic application is best found in the burning passion of the visionaries in your organization.

WHAT IS THE PAYOFF?

The only way to answer this question to the satisfaction of the analytical manager is to estimate the dollar value of the benefits to the organization of the proposed system and subtract the costs of the system. If the resulting figure is healthily positive, few managers will have much to argue with. Even the most intuitive of managers will feel better about the decision to commit to the project if there is a quantitative business case that supports the qualitative benefits of the system.

The way in which this business case is constructed will vary with the organization, the people involved, and the application itself. Traditionally, cost-benefit analyses have been painstaking, time-consuming and controversial, similar to the laborious specification stage associated with traditional information systems development. We have found two general approaches that usually serve well as a template for the business case that is used as a "litmus test" for a strategic application. <u>It should take a relatively short time to construct a thoughtful business case of this type. If the application is at all strategic, major cost savings and organizational benefits should become readily apparent</u>. Note: it is usually easier to measure cost-saving applications than revenue-generating or value-added strategic applications.

TRANSACTION OR ANNUAL APPROACH

The first approach is a transaction-based analysis of the system, based on figuring out how much money the organization makes or saves each time someone queries the SURROUND[SM] system versus how much it costs for that function using previous methods. This approach is most applicable when labor savings are expected to be substantial or critical for an organization's survival. The second approach is to determine the revenues, savings and costs of the SURROUND[SM] system on an annual basis versus the existing methods. In both cases, these figures can be compared with those resulting from doing business without the SURROUND[SM] system, or from taking alternative approaches to building the system.

Medical Professionals' Workstation
Business Case:

PRESENT METHODS   AFTER SURROUND^{SM}

Nurses' Workstation:

TASK:	Total labor cost per day per bed	Total daily labor cost (full hosp.)	Total cost per system (day per bed)	Total daily cost with system (full hospital)	Savings
History & Assesmt.	$5.28	$2,653.00	$2.64	$2,034.00	$618.00
Nursing Care Planning	$6.97	$3,485.00.	$.48	$4,033.83	−$548.63
Interim Assesmt. Activity	$39.28	$19,638.00	$3.18	$16,656.80	$2,981.20
ex. Vit. Sgns.	*$7.14*	*$3,570.00*	*$.60*	*$2,085.00*	*$1,485.00*
Evaluation of Care	$6.12	$3,060.20	$1.62	$810.20	$2,250.00
Medication Admin.	$41.14	$20,570.00	$3.26	$12,037.40	$8,532.60
TOTALS:	$98.79	$49,405.00	$11.16	$35,572.03	$13,833.17

TOTAL PRODUCTIVITY INCREASE PER DAY: $13,833.17
TOTAL PRODUCTIVITY INCREASE PER YEAR: $5,049,107.00

Physicians' Workstation:

TASK:	Total labor cost per day per bed	Total daily labor cost (full hosp.)	Total cost per system (day per bed)	Total daily cost with system (full hospital)	Savings
Preadmission:	$.03	$17.00	$.02	$10.00	$7.00
Admisson: History & Physical	$.68	$340.00	$.70	$350.00	−$10.00

(continued on next page)

Physicians' Workstation (continued):

TASK:	Total daily cost per day per bed	Total daily labor cost (full hosp.)	Total cost per system (day per bed)	Total daily cost with system (full hospital)	Savings
Diagnosis Direct	$.85	$425.00	$.20	$100.00	$325.00
Orders Expert	$70.96	$35,479.00	$9.94	$4,969.00	$7.50
System	$.0	$17.00	$.02	$9.50	$7.50
Hospital Course: Patient Care	$2.04	$1,020.00	$2.26	$1128.50	$(108.50)
Patient List	$.85	$425.00	$.37	$185.00	$240.00
Status Review	$4.25	$2,125.00	$1.05	$525.00	$1,600.00
Results	$1.87	$935.00	$.54	$270.00	$665.00
Consultation	$.51	$255.00	$.14	$71.00	$184.00
Progress Report	$2.04	$1,020.00	$2.07	$1,035.00	$(15.00)
Report Reminders	$.43	$212.50	$.19	$92.50	$120.00
Discharge: Chart Completion:	$1.19	$595.00	$.62	$307.50	$287.50
	$.51	$255.00	$.04	$18.50	$236.50
Quality Assurance:	$3.31	$1,657.50	$1.48	$739.78	$917.72
TOTALS	$89.55	$44,778.00	$19.64	$9,811.00	$34,966.72

TOTAL PRODUCTIVITY TRANSFER PER DAY: **$34,966.72**
TOTAL PRODUCTIVITY TRANSFER PER YEAR: **$12,762.80**

EXAMPLE 1: THE NURSE'S WORKSTATION

As an example of the transaction-oriented approach, take an actual business case constructed for a hospital. This hospital is considering implementing a nurse's workstation system to help cope with the nursing shortage (see sample case on page 77). The case was prepared by examining each of the nurse's tasks addressed by the new system, and comparing the costs of performing each task with and without the system. <u>It is imperative that a business case be developed using figures derived by users of the system.</u>

The pre-system cost of performing a task, such as recording vital signs, primarily consists of labor costs based on the time involved; in the case of recording vital signs, it takes a nurse about 7 minutes to perform the task once for a single patient. Multiplying that by the three times per day a nurse records vital signs at approximately $20 per hour in labor costs leads to a per-bed per-day labor cost of $7.14. Multiplying that figure by the 500 beds in the hospital provides a total hospital cost per day of $3,570 in recording vital signs.

The post-system cost of performing the same task consists of the reduced labor costs—in the case of vital signs that cost is reduced by one-half—plus the cost per transaction of operating the system. This per-transaction cost can be calculated by taking the total cost of operating the system over a two-year period, including hardware, software, communications, training, support, and capital depreciation, and then dividing by the number of minutes in two years to get a per-minute system use cost. Multiplying this per-minute cost by the time the system takes to complete a given task yields the per-transaction cost of 20 cents for recording vital signs.

Thus the post-system cost of recording vital signs is the 20 cent transaction cost plus $1.19 in labor costs, multiplied by three tasks per day and 500 beds in the hospital resulting in a post-system daily hospital cost of $2,085 for recording vital signs. That represents a daily savings of $1,485 over the pre-system costs, or a yearly savings of $542,025. Savings were calculated in a similar way for each of the nurse's tasks addressed by the system, resulting in an anticipated yearly labor cost savings of nearly $10 million with the new system. Other organizations' systems might yield similar savings through reduced training costs, earlier detection of product defects, reduced inventory costs, or any of a thousand different benefits.

<u>Of course, systems benefits don't show up only as savings. Some systems will provide an organization with the ability to add value to its products and services, which can be transformed into higher profit margins and greater market share</u>. In the case of the nurse's workstation system, the hospital planned to add an "expert system" module to check over patient treatment records for possible errors — a value-added application.

The expert system represents a cost rather than a savings to the hospital, since the hospital had nothing comparable to it previously. But if it helps nurses make fewer mistakes, it will result in healthier, more satisfied clients — a value-added benefit. <u>That will lead to increased business, and probably to fewer lawsuits as well</u>. The hospital estimated that the expert system would enhance revenues and reduce lawsuits by a little over $100,000 per year. For other organizations, strategic systems might add value by speeding order turnaround, providing sales reps with better information on customers and products for more effective cross-sells, or by helping a supplier better manage its inventory.

EXAMPLE 2: THE COLLECTOR'S WORKSTATION

Many managers will prefer to see the system costs and benefits analyzed on a yearly basis rather than on a per-transaction basis. As an example, consider the business case for a collector's workstation system designed for a large U.S. city (see sample case on page 83).

This system is intended to help the City reduce its annual rate of uncollected revenues from seven percent to six percent by providing collectors with detailed information on those who owe city taxes and fees such as water bills and parking tickets. In addition, the system would allow the city to reduce the number of collection centers and to reduce the size of the collection staff. The business case quantifies the resulting projected annual savings, along with the one-time cost of the system (the annual operating costs of the system were not expected to add to the city's data processing budget).

Collectors' Workstation Business Case:

A. Higher accounts receivable collection rate

A conservative estimate of 1% improvement in the collections rate (from 7% uncollectible to 6%) of all three revenue centers is used to make a first pass at these numbers. *All figures are in millions of dollars.*

Present Annual Loss from Uncollectibles
Water Resources and Property Taxes Only ($52.500)

Annual Revenue Generation from 1%
Improvement in Collections Rate **$7.500**

B. Reduction in Billing and Collection Costs

1. Collection Centers Reduced from 12 to 8
Annual Cost of Operating Collection Center
s (4)x Cost/Center ($.250)
Annual Savings from Consolidation **$1.000**
2. Reduction in Person Hours Devoted to Collection
# of Person Hours/year (25 @ 2,000 hrs/yr or
50,000 hours x Fully Loaded Hourly Wages of
$15/hour) gives:
Total Annual Personnel Savings **$.750**
3. Reduction in Mailing Costs
Redundant Mailing Eliminated (2)
x Cost/mailing ($.0025)
Total Annual Mail Savings **$.005**

**ESTIMATED TOTAL ANNUAL BENEFIT
(in millions of dollars) $ 9.255**

**ESTIMATED TOTAL COSTS OF IMPLEMENTATION
(in millions of dollars) $ 2.850**

Combined one-time costs for Preliminary and
Production systems hardware and development

PROJECT MANAGEMENT AND REVIEW

The number-laden business case will provide analytical managers with the key information they need to make an initial decision on the project. During and after the project, managers will want to examine project cost figures and time lines and will later check to see if the project is meeting these projections. Hard facts alone often aren't sufficient to gauge the success of the project (any more than they were initially to approve the project). It is often advisable to also rely on the qualitative assessments of key people. For these situations, a critical tool is the project evaluation form—a questionnaire that can be filled out by project leaders, participants and users to rate different aspects of the system's progress (see sample form on page 81).

SAMPLE CLIENT EVALUATION OF SURROUND^{SM} PROJECT

Project Name:_____

Description: _____

Phase:_____
(E = Excellent; G = Good; S = Satisfactory; U = Unacceptable;
N/A = Not applicable)
A. Evaluation of Project Phase
   1.What is your overall evaluation of the system: _____
   2.How well has the SURROUND^{SM} solution helped your
organization better meet its goals: _____
   3.How well does the system help users get their job done:____
   4.How well did the SURROUND^{SM} technological approach
reduce the time and money needed for a project of this size:____
   5.How would you rate the system performance: _____
   6.How well were security requirements met: _____
   7.How well were documentation requirements met: _____
B. How would you rate the SWAT team in the following areas
   1.Technical knowledge: _____
   2.Cooperative and positive attitude: _____
   3.Explanation of technology: _____
   4.Interest in client's needs: _____
   5.Met agreed-upon deliverables: _____
   6.Quality of support during development: _____
C. How would you rate the Supertools
   1.Capabilities and features of Supertools: _____
   2.Ease of use of Supertools: _____
   3.Reliability and maintainability of applications built with
Supertools: _____
Comments:
_____
_____
_____
_____

Evaluation by_____

Name_____Signature_____

Title_____Date_____

These forms will assure managers that the project is meeting its promise, or else identify areas of potential concern. In addition, the forms will present significant evidence to counter the project's inevitable critics who will try to claim that the project is failing to meet its original expectations, or will try to point out failings in the system in time for cancellation. We'll come back to this in Chapter 7.

Now that the business case for a strategic system has been made to the satisfaction of both the intuitive and the analytical manager, it's time to forge ahead with the application. How is it possible to develop a new strategic system rapidly? In the next chapter, we'll take a look at the technologies and methods that can make it happen.

FIRST STEPS

1. Begin to construct a business case for the application that you have identified.

2. List the areas in which you expect to save, how much additional revenue you expect, and why. These could be labor savings, reduced lawsuits, revenues from a business that the new application would enable you to enter, increased revenues re-

sulting from early delivery of the system or "being first."

3. Get the users of the system involved! Form a committee of users whose first mission is to provide you with their ideas on savings and revenue. Who knows better than the user how much time SURROUND^{SM} architecture will save them, or how much more effective they can be with the SURROUND^{SM} system?

4. Make a ballpark estimate of how much it will cost to develop the application, using traditional methods and the SURROUND^{SM} architecture. As a rule of thumb, we have found that the traditional method cost is reduced by 40% to 80% using the SURROUND^{SM} methodology.

5. To avoid endless discussions, do a sensitivity analysis on controversial estimates — most figures by themselves won't make a difference to the bottom line. Instead, find the one or two numbers

in the entire spreadsheet that <u>really</u> do have an impact on the bottom line.

6. Have the users play a key role in building the business case.

V

SUMMARY

· UNIX is a technology that you should consider as a strategic weapon — it frees you from the single vendor, and has "tinkering" capabilities.

· UNIX coupled with business tools currently provides the best foundation on which the SURROUND^{SM} architecture can be built quickly and easily.

· If you choose UNIX it is <u>imperative</u> to add capabilities (which the vendor doesn't provide) for business use, e.g., network management, security, connectivity tools, user interface tools.

Find out at what level and on what applications UNIX is being used in your organization, if at all. Is there any UNIX expertise in your organization right now?

V

The Misunderstood Technology

[UNIX™ is] like selling the Brooklyn Bridge — it's absolutely snake oil.

> Ken Olsen, President
> DEC
> *Digital Review*, March 21, 1988

After this [computer virus problem], I don't see how anyone is ever going to trust UNIX for anything requiring security.

> A Retired Senior IBM Executive
> *Boston Globe*, Nov. 13, 1988

UNIX-based systems provide more opportunity for technological and architectural innovation than other operating systems in its class; AIX will allow IBM to deliver world-class UNIX-based systems to exploit this opportunity.

> Andrew Heller,
> V.P. and Fellow, IBM
> UNIX Expo.

Air Force officials jolted the industry last year when they insisted that any major computer maker plan-

ning to bid on the service's $4.2 billion program to upgrade computer operations — the largest government purchase ever — must provide computers with UNIX operating systems.
New York Times
February 24, 1988

Today, the nearest thing to a vendor-neutral standard for writing software programs is the UNIX operating system ... the number of UNIX-based systems sold has increased more than 70 percent during the past two years, and by the early 1990s UNIX will likely represent more than a quarter of all computer systems sold world-wide.
Wall Street Journal
July 26, 1988

Wait! Don't skip this chapter. Some readers may be tempted to skip this chapter on the assumption that it may be too technical. This chapter is, however, recommended to all readers: it explains some of the key technical issues behind the challenges of strategic information systems without presupposing any familiarity with information systems technology.

THE KEY TO THE SURROUND℠ APPROACH

There are two questions that might occur at this point: What technologies provide the basis for the SURROUND℠ approach? and Why don't MIS departments know about one of these technologies?

Actually, most MIS people do know about it. They just don't realize what they can accomplish with it. It's a little bit like the situation with aspirin— everyone has always known that aspirin can treat headaches, but no one realized it might be able to prevent heart attacks.

<u>There are two keys to SURROUND^{SM} technology. One is special tools for connectivity, security, network management, and performance. The other is a type of software called UNIX™ .</u> Here's the conventional wisdom about UNIX:

- *It is an operating system; that is, it is a software program that coordinates the different hardware components of a computer, like its memory and its disk drives. Software applications programs, such as an accounting system, are usually designed to run with a particular operating system on a particular model of computer.*

- *UNIX's so-called unique features are multitasking and multiuser support — yet virtually all modern operating systems have these.*

- *AT&T wants everybody to use UNIX,*

93

*which suggests it is not well-suited for
IBM, Digital Equipment Corporation
or other vendors' environments.*

· *The government likes UNIX. So do sci-
entists and engineers. It can't do much
for business applications, though.*

All of these statements are misguided. UNIX is
more than an operating system, it offers far more
than portability, it can be applied to virtually any
computer vendor's environment, and it can accomplish near-miracles with business applications. Even
worse than the misconceptions about UNIX is the fact
that almost everyone tends to overlook one of UNIX's
most important features: pipes.

SOFTWARE PLUMBING

A UNIX pipe is a software feature that allows programs to be joined together or "tinkered" together,
treating programs as tinker toys. As a trivial example, imagine a program that computes payroll, and
another one that computes benefits. With UNIX, the
two programs can be piped together; when the first
program is given a name, it will compute payroll and
send the result to the second program, which will
compute bonuses. When the final result is displayed,
it will look as if one program had been at work.

94

That may not sound extraordinary. But bear two things in mind. First of all, other software environments couldn't easily pipe those simple programs together; to combine them in, say, a typical mainframe environment, they would either have to be rewritten as one program, or the results of the first program would have to be put into a batch file or entered manually into the second program (or someone could go through an awkward procedure to come up with a poor imitation of piping).

Secondly, the programs don't have to be trivial, and there can be far more than two. Suppose, for example, that an organization had separate databases for purchase orders and inventory. With pipes, a system could pull out a list from the purchase order database of all the items recently shipped, and have these items automatically deducted from inventory. Without them, unless those programs were originally designed to run together, the information they contain would forever remain separate until someone manually transferred it.*

NON-UNIX TALK

Of course, this is all well and good if programs happen to be running under UNIX. But what if pro-

*For further information, see "Software Cut to Fit" in *UNIX Review*, Dec. 1987, by John J. Donovan.

grams are running under a non-UNIX, proprietary
operating system, a system offered by only a single
vendor (as they almost certainly are)? It's true, programs can't be piped together if they're outside of
UNIX. But there are software tools that allow "reaching in" to other environments, pulling out the needed
information from individual programs, and then
bringing the pieces of information into the UNIX environment where they can be piped together. Thus it
doesn't matter where the programs reside. Here is
the other key to the SURROUND^SM Architecture —
tools. Such "Talk Tools," while they are not standard UNIX, are essential for UNIX to play a role in
your multi-vendor environments.

It's not as difficult as it sounds. Every program
has to communicate with the outside world in some
way. To bring information into UNIX, all a software
tool would have to do is imitate the codes that the
host computer is used to — whether it be a control-
ler, disk, printer, or other device. The program
would be "fooled" into thinking it was talking to the
same device it normally communicates with; it
would accept commands from this Talk Tool and
send the results back to the same Talk Tool residing
in the UNIX environment. Such Talk Tools do exist,
e.g., Talksna™ Talkasync ™ , etc.

96

The UNIX environment itself can be running on a small computer thousands of miles away, communicating by phone line to the computers running the main programs, or it can be running on the same computer as the main programs (IBM's VM and other vendors' computers will simultaneously support UNIX along with their standard operating systems). Either way, once the Talk Tool has brought the needed information into UNIX, UNIX pipes allow the information to be combined and compared as required.

INTERFACE TOOLS

The results can then be connected with a special interface —such as a touch-tone phone interface or a personal computer interface (like the one used in the Mormon Church's application). While such interface tools are not part of UNIX, they are enhanced in this environment.

The key to the SURROUND^{SM} architecture is a UNIX environment plus a series of special software tools for bringing information in and out of UNIX, where the information can be piped into Network Management Tools such as DataHandler™ and Interface™ . The UNIX environment and the Talk Tools are the bridge between the existing systems that contain the needed information and the interfaces with which the people using the application interact. Without UNIX the SURROUND^{SM} architecture would be virtually impossible. With UNIX and the software tools the SURROUND^{SM} architecture seems almost trivial.

A CLOSER LOOK AT UNIX

How could UNIX's capabilities be so overlooked by the computer industry and MIS departments? Actually, UNIX does have its fans, particularly among technical and government users. Business is beginning to catch on, too. Seven percent of all the money spent on computers and software in 1986 went into the UNIX environment and machines to support it, according to research firm International Data Corporation. IDC predicts that share will grow to 22 percent by 1991. In contrast, IBM's premier environment, the 370 architecture, has been losing market share.

But even UNIX's biggest supporters tend to underutilize the environment's best features. They only use UNIX's standard operating system features, which is somewhat like stepping into the cockpit of a jet plane and driving it at 55 miles-per-hour down a highway. The most common oversight made by UNIX users is not taking full advantage of UNIX's pipes. Beware! Even some of the major vendors supporting UNIX produce programs that cannot be piped.

Incredibly, being oblivious to UNIX's unique strength is the rule, rather than the exception, within the UNIX side of the computer industry. While organizations are desperately in need of the ability to integrate their different systems, everyone is ignoring the ultimate integration tool—and it's sitting right under their noses.

NOT JUST AN OPERATING SYSTEM*

Piping isn't the only valuable feature UNIX has. UNIX provides, for example, an extensive collection of software "utilities" or special programs that speed programming tasks. <u>It also offers a built-in fourth-generation language called "Shell" that allows users to specify complicated commands in a few words</u>.

Of course, other environments offer a wide range of powerful programming utilities and fourth generation languages. However, with the UNIX environment's pipes, these features take on special significance. Pipes allow any tool or Shell program to be instantly accessed at any point within any other program. Piping therefore endows standard tools with extraordinary powers.

*For additional information on operating systems, see John J. Donovan and Stuart E. Madnick, *Operating Systems*, MacGraw-Hill, 1974.

WHERE CAN YOU GO?

UNIX's portability is also increasingly becoming a crucial feature. Portability allows a program to be moved from any computer running UNIX and to any other computer running UNIX. Nearly all vendors are offering UNIX on their computers regardless of the computer's size or manufacturer. That means organizations are never locked into any particular vendor's computers. That's a big advantage, considering that these days each vendor seems to provide one piece of the computing puzzle, with no one vendor able to provide a complete solution.

The SURROUND^{SM} architecture capitalizes on the usefulness of UNIX's portability. That's because the SURROUND^{SM} environment can quickly and significantly increase in size as additional interfaces and existing systems are brought into a strategic application. Thus, the SURROUND^{SM} environment might at first fit onto a personal computer and end up requiring a large minicomputer a few months later. UNIX's portability ensures that a variety of different-sized computers can be enlisted to handle the job, without necessitating a costly conversion of the SURROUND^{SM} software.

100

WHY TALK TOOLS IN A
UNIX ENVIRONMENT?

Connectivity tools running in non-UNIX environments generally only connect to one system at a time. If the information needed is scattered among several systems, the systems have to be dialed up one at a time. The Talk Tools, by comparison, can simultaneously connect the SURROUND^{SM} environment to an unlimited number of systems. Also, unlike the Talk Tools, tools running in non-UNIX environments aren't easily customizable to any other environment. Connecting to an environment other than the one the tool was specifically designed for requires buying a different tool, which will entail learning a new set of commands.

Even if a tool can be made to work with a given non-UNIX environment, it still won't translate information from one application to another. To do so, someone will have to know how to manually reformat the information so it will be acceptable to each different application. A few vendors sell automatic reformatting packages but these products, which are expensive and difficult to install, typically work with only a few specialized types of applications.

The two main shortcomings of these tools running in a non-UNIX environment is that they can't be

<u>piped</u> between a new application and an existing application to integrate the two, <u>and they are limited to certain manufacturers' environments</u>. Instead, these tools can only pass information between applications under manual control or with files. Clearly, such tools don't even come close to providing the automatic connectivity that is needed to build a SURROUND^{SM} environment.

SPEAKING THE SAME LANGUAGE

Computer systems vendors are talking a lot about connectivity these days. <u>Beware, though: most computer vendors and others are struggling merely to provide "hardware connectivity" between each other's (and sometimes their own) systems</u>. Hardware connectivity allows two systems to talk to one another, but that doesn't mean that the systems will understand each other. It's analogous to the person-to-person connectivity provided by a telephone: it's not very useful to an American to be able to call Japan if neither party speaks a common language.

In the case of an international phone call, what's needed is a translator included in the call to act as an intermediary between both ends of the conversation. In the case of two incompatible computer systems trying to communicate, an intermediary is also needed to allow the different applications to understand each other. Computer vendors can't provide this "applications" connectivity between dissimilar machines. But a SURROUND^{SM} environment armed with Talk Tools can.

The SURROUND^{SM} environment will also accommodate new tools being created in the industry now. Several organizations are currently working to establish software standards that will eventually provide full connectivity. The International Standards Organization, for example, is hammering out the much-acclaimed "LU6.2" standard, while IBM is pushing for its "System Applications Architecture" standard. Complete working specifications for these and other standards are still years away, and even then incorporating the standards will require extensive rewriting of applications.

Eventually, such standards will enable unlike applications to communicate. In many cases this will remove the need to rely on the application translation capabilities of the Talk Tools, which will then simply operate more efficiently. In the meantime, the Talk-Tool-equipped SURROUND^{SM} environment provides the only practical means to achieve applications connectivity across a range of systems — vendors' claims notwithstanding.

WHY UNIX?

To sum up, UNIX pipes and filters allow utilities, programs and even entire applications running under UNIX to be joined together instantly. The Supertools extend this ability to outside the UNIX environment. These are the secrets of the SURROUND^{SM} environment's ability to link existing applications and transform them into a strategic application. They help explain why a major strategic application that might be impossible to build in a typical environment can be built in weeks using the SURROUND^{SM} technology.

UNIX by itself is not enough. It must be supplemented by Supertools to provide security, network management, and connectivity to be applied to your strategic system.

FIRST STEPS:

1. Beware. Your traditional technical people may object to using UNIX. Don't give up — it is too important to your future.

2. All major advances in computing today, e.g., ex-

pert systems, parallel processing, and advanced user interfaces are being implemented primarily in UNIX environments.

3. Are there applications on disparate systems from which you would like to integrate information but, again, have not been able to? Consider UNIX and the Talk Tools.

4. Get with it — order a UNIX machine. Start getting your staff familiarized with this important technology.

5. Supplement UNIX with network management, security, and connectivity tools from third-party software vendors.

6. Develop internal expertise in UNIX. See the list of additional readings at the end of the book for suggestions.

VI

SUMMARY

- The SWAT team approach can completely change the way organizations view information technology.

- The key to building a system that meets the strategic needs of the organization is to make sure it is driven by users and strategic planners.

- SWAT teams are much smaller than traditional development teams and they consist primarily of organizational leaders and people who will use the system.

- Supertools provide the critical ability for user involvement and astounding gains in the productivity of your technical people.

- The Preliminary System Architecture provides a "prefabricated" generic strategic application architecture.

VI

The Preliminary System

Technical people must find a way to give users what they want. The SURROUND^SM technology definitely plays a role in any business that's looking to level the playing field.

> Ron Cipolla, Dir., MIS
> Kendall Hospital Supply

The users design the system that <u>they</u> want. And they get it <u>now</u>, not six months or a year or a year and a half from now.

> Steve Masie, Supervisor
> Textron Lycoming

Once a strategic application has been identified, the development process can begin. We break the process up into two major phases — preliminary and production — and a number of sub-phases. For strategic applications, we've found the preliminary phase to be a critical step in the process. It takes five days.

How can anyone build a strategic application — even if it's a preliminary version — in just one week? But what are your options? Can you keep users involved in development for more than a week? And if it's strategic, when do you need it?

HOW IN ONE WEEK?

We've already discussed part of the answer: the process is based on the SURROUND℠ architecture, which is in turn based on UNIX's integration capabilities and the Supertools' ability to bring information in and out of the UNIX environment. But there are two other keys: one is the "Special Weapons and Tactics" (SWAT) team approach and the other is the Preliminary System Architecture based on the SURROUND℠ approach, which provides a framework that cuts out the time-consuming drudgery usually involved in application development. We've adapted this SWAT team approach to the process, which will maximize the speed, organizational support and strategic thinking that goes into the effort.

The traditional application building process is tedious, frustrating and highly technical. On the other hand, this one–week, flat–out assault is exciting and highly rewarding — and is aimed primarily at non-technical business managers. <u>It can completely change the way organizations view information technology.</u>

PRELIMINARY VS. PRODUCTION

The resulting preliminary system won't be in its final form. Rather, it will be a "preliminary" system that will lack some of the features necessary in a large-scale application, such as security and the power to handle hundreds of users. But don't mistake the preliminary system for a "prototype" system you might be familiar with. Prototypes are generally hastily built "fake" applications based on a single database that merely simulate the functionality of a real system to provide people with a rough idea of what the application might eventually look like. <u>The preliminary system we're building, on the other hand, will be an actual, functioning application capable of tying into existing systems.</u>

Turning the preliminary system into a finished, "production" application is a separate process that takes about three to five months (we'll cover this process in the next chapter). Why build two different versions of the same application? Because even though the several-month production system process is phenomenally fast by traditional MIS standards, it's still too long and involved to be <u>driven by users and strategic planners</u> —which is the key to ending up with a system that meets the strategic needs of the organization.

Building a separate preliminary version first speeds up, simplifies and focuses the process to the point where a team of primarily non-technical managers can construct the most strategic elements of the system in one week. The preliminary system then serves as a detailed outline to be filled in by the production system building process.

ASSEMBLING A SWAT TEAM

In the conventional application-building process, the development team consists almost entirely of MIS technical people — as many as hundreds of them if it's a major application. Top organizational managers and people who will use the system provide various degrees of input into the process, typically a "user specifications document," but rarely do such MIS "outsiders" directly participate in the building of the application.

The SWAT-style development team differs in two fundamental ways. First of all, SWAT teams are much smaller than traditional development teams. Secondly, SWAT teams consist primarily of organizational leaders and people who will use the system. Where will the technical expertise needed to build a strategic application come from?

That's the whole point of the Preliminary System Architecture — it allows people who don't know anything about computers (but who do know a lot about what the organization's needs are) to drive the process. These non-technical people are leveraged by the Supertools and UNIX.

Limiting the number of people on the team is crucial to achieving SWAT team effectiveness. Larger groups spend much of their energy ironing out administrative and political details and rarely manage to retain a strong sense of mission. In addition, the application development process almost always involves turning up unforeseen challenges along the way. A large group of technicians will tend to push such unanticipated factors off to the side as it plods towards an unchanging goal. A SWAT team, on the other hand, can take advantage of its size and business expertise to quickly overcome unexpected bar-

111

riers and take advantage of the unexpected opportunities.

TEAM LEADERSHIP

<u>Loading the team with managers and users is also crucial</u>. The managers can keep the team focused on the strategic goals, and recognize ways that the project can address additional strategic issues. Users will make sure that the finished application is one that meets their needs, as well as one that they are comfortable dealing with. When a traditional technical team develops an application, managers and users are usually unpleasantly surprised at the ways in which the results fall short of their expectations. But when managers and users drive the development process, they feel a sense of ownership and are justifiably proud of the finished application; not only will they use it, but they will help sell it to the rest of the organization.

That's not to say that technical people are barred from the team. Indeed, they are crucial to the project, because they know the ins and outs of the existing systems to which the new application will be connecting. But having three or four technical people working side-by-side with managers and users is a very different situation from having 250 technical people working off on their own. On the SWAT team,

112

the technicians' efforts will be precisely directed at the overall strategic needs of the organization and the more specific needs of the people who will be using the system.

In addition to MIS technicians, the team must also include two or three people who have had some exposure to the SURROUND^{SM} architecture, either through formal training or past participation in a SURROUND^{SM} project. These SURROUND^{SM} technology experts will help guide the rest of the team through the use of the Architecture and the associated Tools.

BUILDING A GREENHOUSE

<u>Once you've identified your SWAT team, you'll need to create a "greenhouse" to protect the team from hostile elements and nurture its growth</u>. Choose facilities as isolated as possible from everyone's normal work environment to avoid the day–to–day distractions of the office. The team needs to feel that their efforts are being recognized as important to the organization and given adequate resources and attention.

Bringing in third-party consultants can be beneficial for providing a fresh viewpoint; however, be wary of vendors that promise to provide the "total solution." Their primary interest is not in achieving

113

goals of your organization, but rather in maximizing the sales of *their* organization.

The environment you want to create is a "can-do" environment, so it's important to protect the team from naysayers in your organization. It's a little bit like the fisherman who doesn't bother to put a lid on a basket of crabs that he's caught. He doesn't need to because as soon as one crab tries to escape to freedom by climbing out of the basket, another one will pull the first crab back. <u>Don't let the crabs get to you or your team!</u> "Crabs" will give you all the reasons why things *won't* work, rather than how to *make* them work.

Since setting up a SWAT team is highly visible, you run the risk of alienating the rest of your staff by creating a two-tiered structure. <u>To avoid alienation, rotate your people in and out of the SWAT team.</u> You'll build a bigger team, have better distribution of knowledge and break down barriers between different groups in your organization.

THE PROCESS

In five days, your SWAT team can take an identified strategic application, define it, and build a preliminary version of it. The users should drive this process, defining and refining the application, rechecking its relevance to your organization's goals

114

and critical success factors, and actually building the user interfaces as they'd like to see them. They should take the preliminary business case you developed in Chapter 4 and work on fleshing it out to an additional level of detail. Your investment in the identified application thus far has been minimal and chances are you'll still want to have a convincing case for proceeding to the production stage described in Chapter 7.

The technical people should work on building the parts of the system behind the user interface (e.g., the connectivity, the databases, the data flows, etc.). Typically, these pieces can be developed in parallel, with frequent checkpoints between these parallel efforts.

A key element to the process is the use of Supertools. Users should be able to build interfaces with minimal training and frustration and the technical people should have tools that increase their productivity by several orders of magnitude. In addition to the Supertools, we've found our Preliminary System Architecture to be a key component of the process.

THE PRELIMINARY SYSTEM ARCHITECTURE

Complex strategic applications can't be thrown together. They require a carefully thought out structure, or architecture. That's true when using the SURROUND^{SM} approach as well, but there's a twist that eliminates the considerable task of designing and building a custom architecture. The SURROUND^{SM} approach uses a "prefabricated," generic strategic application architecture, called the Preliminary System Architecture.

Just as with a prefabricated home, all that remains to be done with the Preliminary System Architecture is to customize it and add the trim. Despite the ready-made design, the finished strategic application will look and perform precisely as required for the specific application; it will be indistinguishable from one that was painstakingly built from scratch.

The Preliminary System Architecture is a sort of "Megatool," in that it incorporates a number of Supertools, such as the Talk Tools described in the last chapter. The overall Preliminary System Architecture is shown in Figure 1. Implementing the architecture simply involves letting the Supertools guide the SWAT team through the customization process.

116

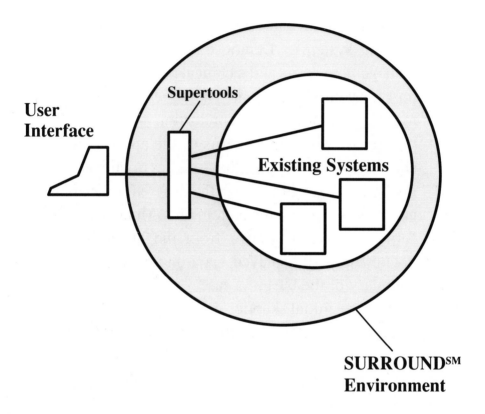

Figure 1
The Preliminary System Architecture

"SELLING" THE SYSTEM

At the end of this intensive development, you'll have a working preliminary system that *shows* the actual "look and feel" of the system and demonstrates the ability to establish connectivity to your existing systems. Demonstrate the system to top management, users and technical people to gain support for your application. <u>The system is a valuable tool for you to "sell" the application — use it!</u> Emphasize the strategic benefits of the application by showing how the application satisfies organizational goals and CSFs. Emphasize the difference the application will make on the bottom line. Much of this information can be drawn from the business case document, and displayed via a one-page executive summary of the business case.

Despite initial skepticism, a small team has built a major strategic application in one week and sold it to top management as well. Now let's look at what has to be done to get the application up and running in its finished form.

FIRST STEPS

1. Identify a SWAT team for developing the strategic application you've identified. Who will be the business/ user leaders? Who will be the technical

leaders?

2. Find a separate physical location at which you plan to build your greenhouse.
   – Pick a location that is conducive to users and technologists
   – Do not build it in a computer vendor setting.

3. Build your preliminary system, using UNIX Super-tools and the Preliminary System Architecture.

4. Refine the business case you developed in Chapter 3.

5. Demonstrate your system to top management and get buy-off for the next step — building the production version.

6. You control the hardware vendors — your system is portable. Look for service, amiability and cooperation as differentiation characteristics.

VII

SUMMARY

- Using the SURROUND^{SM} technology, production systems typically take 10 to 19 weeks to implement, as opposed to 1 to 6 years with traditional approaches.

- The key to building the production version lies in the prefabricated SURROUND^{SM} architecture and the SWAT team approach.

- By utilizing the SURROUND^{SM} methodology and UNIX, you have redefined the rules for determining your hardware platform.

- A truly strategic system must be a living, growing entity, if it is to continue to meet the organization's needs, create new opportunities and stay ahead of competitors.

- The SURROUND^{SM} approach provides an organiza-

tion with two long–term options: the SUR-
ROUND^{SM} environment and the original systems can
be replaced with an entirely new system built from
scratch; or, the SURROUND^{SM} environment can be
expanded and restructured to "absorb" and replace
the existing systems.

**Reevaluate the value of the strategic application
you prototyped in Chapter 6. Does it meet the goals
and CSFs of the organization? Does your business
case justify taking it into production? Continue to
sell the SWAT team concept within your organization
as a company–wide resource for developing the
most strategic applications.**

VII

The Production System — Reality

Every business has a thrust to put technology in the hands of the client. When we used to hear that in a strategy, we would groan and say "How?". We saw it done here — not only done, but done in a manner that allows the clients to sit down, understand and visualize. It's tremendous.

> Jan Kwasniak, V.P.
> CIGNA

This has truly been a technological feat to develop a fully operational production system in this time schedule.

> John Heinz, V.P.
> MNC Info. Svcs., subsidiary of
> Maryland National Bank.

The [SURROUND^{SM} system] is absolutely critical — I <u>can't</u> wait until 1992 for it.

> William Sanders, Gen. Mgr.
> Inland Steel Company

Why not just run the preliminary system as a finished version?

122

Actually, it could be done. The preliminary system is a legitimate strategic application that provides most of the capabilities the organization is looking for. However, turning it over to the organization to run on a daily basis would lead to several problems.

For one thing, the preliminary system was designed to be used by a handful of people; by now there may be hundreds of people who need to get their hands on it. For another, the SWAT team probably never had a chance to build in all the "important but non-critical" features it had listed, and since then people have probably thought of even more features they'd like to see the system handle.

The preliminary system is also slow; it may take twenty seconds or more to carry out a function, a delay that would drive users crazy in constant use. Finally, the preliminary system has few security or data integrity features. That means that the system could be fouled up by an improper command or a noisy telephone line, and that unauthorized users could browse through and even change the data in the system.

With these issues in mind, we're now going to build a more powerful, more complete, more "bullet-proof" version of the preliminary system, which we'll call the "production" version. It will take about two to four months to complete it. If that seems like a long time, compare it to the traditional MIS process:

TRADITIONAL APPROACH

PHASE	TIME TO COMPLETE
Prototype	1 to 6 months
Final user Specifications	1 to 6 months
System Design	3 months to 1year
Coding	6 months to 3 years
Testing and revision	3 months to one year

Total time: 1 to 6 years

SURROUND℠ APPROACH

PHASE	TIME TO COMPLETE
Preliminary System	1 week
Production System	9 to 18 weeks

Total time: 10 to 19 weeks

That's quite a difference in time. But there are other differences, too. Traditional prototypes are extremely limited programs that simulate the required functionality of a very simple (and thus probably non-strategic) application. Most prototypes can't, for example, tie together two similar systems running on the same computer, never mind a half-dozen dissimilar systems running on different computers. After a prototype is built, it's thrown away and the MIS department does the best it can to incorporate

124

some of the prototype's functionality into the real application.

The SURROUND^{SM} -based preliminary system, on the other hand, is a sophisticated but no-frills version of the production system. Anything the preliminary system can do (which is quite a bit), the production version will do and more. In fact, much of the work done on the preliminary system can be applied to the production system, providing an enormous head start.

THE SAME KEY TO SUCCESS

The process of building a production system parallels that of building a preliminary system. Once again, the key is a prefabricated SURROUND^{SM} architecture, and a SWAT team approach.

The Production System Architecture, like the Preliminary System Architecture, eliminates the long and difficult process of developing a system architecture from scratch. The Architecture consists of modules that need only be customized to provide all the capabilities required for the strategic application. The Production System Architecture modules are more sophisticated than their preliminary counterparts, and provide a correspondingly higher level of performance, functionality and flexibility.

125

The SWAT team approach for production systems is likewise similar to the preliminary systems approach in that a relatively small, highly focused team of users and technical experts customizes a set of almost-ready-to-run Supertools. But it also differs in some important ways. The most obvious of these is that it takes ten weeks instead of one; another is that it requires more technical expertise.

Transforming a preliminary system into a production system is more than a trivial exercise. As an example, let's look at an actual preliminary system and see what enhancements are required for the production system.

THE ISSUES

As an example, let's take a major supplier of blood products that built a national blood inventory system designed to link 56 regions together. In addition, 3000 hospitals would remotely tie in to these 56 centers. They built their preliminary system in 1 week and their production system in 14 weeks.

The preliminary system works well, but a number of improvements are required for a production version. Here's a comparison of the two:

PRELIMINARY SYSTEM FEATURES	PRODUCTION SYSTEM FEATURES
1. Takes 10 seconds to update inventory	Must take less than 1 second to update inventory
2. Supports 2 users	Supports 3000 hospital users with remote access
3. Has access to three external systems	Has access to data from 56 regional systems and hundreds of hospital systems
4. Anyone can access the system	Denies access to the system unauthorized users, stops improper modification, has security
5. System has no error handling	Handles errors
6. Has limited functionality	Has full working functionality
7. No maintenance or network management	Must have maintenance and network management
8. Short-term development	Need management of production process over time
9. Hardware platform irrelevant	Must determine final hardware platform

We'll describe how we address each of these issues in the following sections.

MEETING PERFORMANCE REQUIREMENTS

The performance goal is to reduce the time a user waits for the system to respond. The preliminary system tools are replaced by the production system tools. Some reduction is automatically provided by the new tools, which are designed to run faster than their preliminary counterparts. The coordination module can be customized to minimize bottlenecks, and ensure that other modules aren't sitting idle. If the SURROUND^{SM} computer is still getting bogged down, certain pieces of one or more modules can simply be ported to a larger computer or distributed among multiple computers.

In some cases, response time will be held up by delays in outside systems beyond the team's control. A way to deal with these delays is to provide additional functions to the user. This might involve prompting the user for another request or for more information, or perhaps simply providing a message that might be of interest such as a sales promotion. Though such actions won't speed up the system, they can reduce the "perceived" response time to the point where it is no longer seen as a problem.

128

Another solution to the problem of outside system delays is to bring the outside database (or key pieces of it) into the SURROUND^{SM} environment, in effect operating as part of the local data processing module. Transporting a large, non-UNIX database into the SURROUND^{SM} environment is usually a chore beyond the scope of the immediate project, but such moves should be considered later for their long-range benefits.

Other technical issues, such as Issues 2–6, can be addressed by layering production tools to replace the prototyping tools on the SURROUND^{SM} computer. These tools will provide for error handling, security and allow the users to increase the functionality of their systems.

APPLICATION NETWORK MANAGEMENT

The production version of your SUR-ROUND^{SM} system will require adequate attention by both users of the system and the technical people assigned to maintain the system. The dependence of the system on outside systems begs the question: "What happens to my system when these outside applications change?" <u>Network management tools play a key role in managing your SURROUND^{SM} system</u>. At this time neither UNIX nor the vendors have such tools. This important issue of applications network management will be addressed in the next chapter.

PROJECT MANAGEMENT

You probably won't have the luxury of full-time users on the SWAT team as you did in the preliminary system development; however, it is important to maintain their involvement in the project. <u>Frequent deliverables (e.g. in a 12-week project, you might have three deliverables, at 4 weeks, 8 weeks and 12 weeks into the project), and weekly checkpoints with key users are a key to success.</u> Measure your team's effectiveness using evaluation forms that rate user satisfaction of the project as it progresses (see sample form).

Even after the system is successfully completed, you may run into skeptics, or "crabs." The evaluation forms will help you to state your (successful) case, or discover substantive problems you need to correct.

SAMPLE CLIENT EVALUATION OF SURROUND^{SM} PROJECT

Project Name:_____

Description: _____

Phase:_____
(E = Excellent; G = Good; S = Satisfactory; U = Unacceptable; N/A = Not applicable)

A. Evaluation of Project Phase
   1.What is your overall evaluation of the system: _____
   2.How well has the SURROUND^{SM} solution helped your organization better meet its goals: _____
   3.How well does the system help users get their job done:____
   4.How well did the SURROUND^{SM} technological approach reduce the time and money needed for a project of this size:____
   5.How would you rate the system performance: _____
   6.How well were security requirements met: _____
   7.How well were documentation requirements met: _____
B. How would you rate the SWAT team in the following areas
   1.Technical knowledge:
   2.Cooperative and positive attitude: _____
   3.Explanation of technology: _____
   4.Interest in client's needs: _____
   5.Met agreed-upon deliverables: _____
   6.Quality of support during development: _____
C. How would you rate the Supertools
   1.Capabilities and features of Supertools: _____
   2.Ease of use of Supertools: _____
   3.Reliability and maintainability of applications built with Supertools: _____
Comments:
_____
_____
_____
_____

Evaluation by_____

Name_____Signature_____

Title_____Date_____

CHOOSING A HARDWARE VENDOR

By choosing the SURROUND^{SM} methodology and UNIX, you have redefined the rules for determining your hardware platform. Because UNIX is an industry standard, most vendors can offer you a platform on various-sized computers.

You can then issue a "Request for Proposal" (RFP) to a number of vendors for fulfilling your complete hardware needs and have the ability to compare the prices, processing power, and service of various vendors. Having these alternatives then puts you in a better position to negotiate the best package for your organization. You may even choose to split the bid among several vendors, decreasing your dependence on any one vendor.

PILOT TEST

As the system nears completion, its components should be tested and integrated. When the entire application is more or less functional, you can begin the pilot test phase. The pilot test puts a few users on the system in a controlled environment (where it can't affect critical operations) to shake out bugs and make final recommendations. It doesn't have to take long, but should be done before the system is actually rolled out to full deployment.

MAXIMIZING AND MAINTAINING THE BENEFITS

Even if the system is living up to its strategic promise, it would be a mistake to assume it's a finished product. That's because three things are going to happen: first, the strategic needs of the organization will change, sometimes drastically; second, the beneficiaries of the system, including users, managers, customers and suppliers, will start to come up with new ideas of what they want; and finally, if the system meets its potential then it's safe to assume that competitors will be only a half step behind, at best, in rolling out their own efforts.

<u>Thus a truly strategic system must be a living, growing entity if it is to continue to meet the organization's needs, create new opportunities, and stay ahead of competitors.</u> American Airlines' SABRE reservation system—one of the first and best known strategic applications—has long since become a dynamic business in its own right, having expanded into hotel and rental car reservations, and even into helping track travel and entertainment expenses.

FREQUENT ENHANCEMENTS

Implementing new opportunities and needed changes in a strategic application is far easier in the SURROUND^{SM} environment than with more tradi-

133

tional approaches. New interfaces and functionality can be added at will, without extensive rewriting of existing programs. When the American Red Cross invited a dozen hospitals to examine its new blood-ordering application, the hospitals came up with 72 suggested additions and modifications to the system. The Red Cross was able to incorporate these changes into the SURROUND^{SM} environment in a few weeks. Additional existing databases can be plugged into the SURROUND^{SM} environment in hours, and completely new databases can be built into the SUR-ROUND^{SM} environment in days.

To take advantage of the SURROUND^{SM} -based application's ability to meet even greater user and organizational needs, the organization must ensure that the appropriate people are attentive to watching out for new requirements and opportunities. The simplest way to do so is to <u>bring the managers and SWAT team members involved in the original project together on a regular basis—perhaps once a week for the first few months after the system is rolled out, and then once a month throughout the first year</u>. Eventually the team might meet bimonthly or quarterly throughout the life of the application.

Managers and team members ideally arrive at these meetings prepared with ideas for enhancing the system; these ideas can come from user group meetings, electronic suggestion boxes, customer input delivered by sales people, interviews with senior managers, competitive research, or from any number of other sources. Whenever possible, the team should invite potential idea-generators to meetings to provide direct input.

GOALS AND CSFs REVISITED

A good starting point for team meetings is to re-visit the Goals and Critical Success Factors method that was employed to target the original strategic application idea. The team can determine if goals have changed, or if new goals are emerging; CSFs can then be determined accordingly, and ideas for adapting or enhancing the strategic application will flow naturally from these.

At Chrysler in the early 1980s, for example, the goal of the near-bankrupt organization was clearly survival, and a CSF was maintaining cash flow. If Chrysler had decided to build a strategic application intended to address this CSF, it might have applied the SURROUND^{SM} architecture to its various dealership and supplier accounting systems to determine its balance of payments on a given day. A few years later, Chrysler was out of its money crunch; its new goal was market share, and the primary CSF was im-

135

proving the quality of its cars. To adapt the strategic system to its new CSF, the company might have added a defect tracking database to its dealership and supplier tie-ins.

EVOLUTION OF AN APPLICATION

As an organization continues to modify and expand a SURROUND^{SM}-based application, a point might be reached where it makes sense to consider restructuring the application and replacing the original systems which supply the new application with its data. That might be due to performance or flexibility limitations of the existing systems which might be limiting the strategic application's scope, or it might be because the SURROUND^{SM} environment has grown to the point where the original systems have become a relatively small part of the application.

In either case, the SURROUND^{SM} technology provides an organization with two options: both the SURROUND^{SM} environment and the original systems can be replaced with an entirely new, integrated strategic system built from scratch; or, the SURROUND^{SM} environment can be expanded and restructured to "absorb" and replace the existing systems, so that the SURROUND^{SM} environment comprises the entire application.

The extreme flexibility of the SURROUND^{SM} environment makes the latter option a wise choice in most circumstances, especially in cases where the SURROUND^{SM} environment has already grown to incorporate most of the application. However, some organizations' MIS departments will simply be too committed to traditional technologies to make the transition to an all new environment, no matter what the advantages. These organizations can then use the SURROUND^{SM} environment as a strategic bridge between original and new applications; the SURROUND^{SM} environment and the original systems can be replaced piece by piece using conventional technologies, until a new, integrated application based on traditional approaches is in place.

In many cases, evolving organizational goals require an entirely separate application rather than just a modification or expansion of an existing strategic application. To ensure that as many of these opportunities as possible are being identified and implemented and that each application is reaching its full potential, organizations should take steps to institutionalize the necessary attitudes, methodologies and technologies. We'll discuss ways of doing so in Chapter Nine. But first we'll tackle the increasingly crucial challenge of managing strategic computer networks.

FIRST STEPS

1. Prepare for developing the production version of the preliminary system you developed in Chapter 6. Assemble your SWAT team and identify objectives for them. Designate technical and user leaders.

2. Have the team design the system and put together a detailed project plan.

3. Have the team build the production system. Use client evaluation forms to manage the development process.

4. Write an RFP and submit it to multiple vendors.

5. Set up a forum for continual evaluation of the system by users and technical people. Designate resources for maximizing and maintaining the benefits of the system on an on-going basis.

6. Determine your long-term strategy for the system. Do you want to eventually "pillage and burn" the SURROUND^{SM} environment and your existing sys-

tems? Or do you want the SURROUND^{SM} environment to gradually "absorb" your existing systems?

VIII

SUMMARY

Wait! When we say "network management," we do not simply mean what the telephone companies say: managing the wire. There are three levels that must be managed:

1. **The physical level:** If modems and other communications equipment fail, you have a problem. Managing that failure means rerouting the information around the failed *physical* components.

2. **The system level:** Do you know when the computers on your network are about to become overloaded? Can you monitor the performance of every machine on the network? These are the *systems-level* management questions.

3. **The application level:** What happens if the wires are still connected, the performance is fine, but someone changes one of the applications? Can you detect such *application* changes and can you take the appropriate actions?

VIII

Managing The Strategic Network

Our network must never go down, not just for competitive reasons, but because the health of American people is at stake.

> Maribeth Luftglass,
> Assoc. Dir., Telecommunications
> American Red Cross

Every second our network is down, it's dollars ticking by.

> Howard Kolodny, President
> The Cambridge Funds

TACTICAL TO STRATEGIC

The Good News: You've implemented your dream.
The Bad News: If your network fails, without the appropriate network management tools, your dream can become a nightmare.

So your tactical systems have now been made strategic by networking. But have you been led down a grassy path, simply to find that this beautiful lane ends in a sheer cliff? No!

141

WHAT CAN FAIL?

The Physical Level: Problems and Solutions

Among the various physical network pieces that can fail are phone lines, modems, controllers and the like. There are numerous hardware and software products designed to watch over these and other components, alerting network administrators when a component has failed. Tools such as AT&T's Dataphone II™ and IBM's NetView™ do well at diagnosing physical component problems.

The Systems Level: Problems but Fewer Solutions

What happens if the hardware does not fail, but the computers are overloaded? Can you monitor performance throughout the network? The answer is:

- · YES — If you have an all-IBM network, NetView™ can help you.

- · YES — If you have an all-DEC network, DECnet™ can help you.

- · MAYBE — Some environments, such as UNIX, have no vendor-supported network management capabilities. Third party vendors may offer such network management tools.

· NO — If you have a multi-vendor network.

Currently available vendor products do not offer methods for managing at the system level such problems as performance, database overflow, and remote testing and distribution of software across *heterogeneous* networks.

There is a way around this problem, and the answer lies in the SURROUND^{SM} architecture. Utilizing the CAMBRIDGE METHOD^{SM}, a major U.S. manufacturer decided that while each of their present network management tools was good for its specific job, *critical* to their business was an integrated system, with the ability to alert operators of any network problem, *regardless of manufacturer*. The loss of their network at a given time could result in losses in excess of $100,000 per hour! The revenue increases in having reliable network management amounted to hundreds of millions of dollars per year in bottom-line profit.

A SURROUND^{SM} system was created to integrate the disparate network management software, including IBM's NetView™ running on an IBM mainframe,

Uccel's Netman™ , also running on an IBM main-frame, Digital's DECnet™ running on DEC VAX machines, and GDC's Netcon™ running on PCs. The system presents the network operators with a unified view of the network, and pinpoints the specific trouble location on demand. The heterogeneous network management system (at the system level) even takes care of trouble log entries and, in some cases, reduces total trouble response time by 83% !

THE APPLICATION LEVEL

Problem: Application Changes Affect the Network

You have linked your applications together (e.g. with your suppliers and customers) to form a strategic advantage. What is the likelihood that some customer, some supplier, some division, or someone else on the network, will make a change to their core application? The Bank of Boston, for example, introduces an average of 250 changes in its applications software every week. What happens to your single interface if some independent supplier on the network changes its application — e.g. changes a password? Conventional network management tools offer no means for coping with such alterations.

144

For example, imagine a brokerage house were to develop a world-wide trading system by connecting together their national offices, thus producing top-level summary information in a single "Executive Spreadsheet." If the London office were to, say, begin transmitting in dollars instead of pounds as a "favor" to the headquarters, what would happen to the application?

At this point the communications companies would say that the network is completely intact. In fact, the systems-level network management programs would also confirm this fact. But the *user* would find that his figures had jumped to a different range, and would realize quickly that *his* network was broken!

The Traditional Solution

The traditional solution to avoiding surprise applications changes, is to dictate a policy to all people capable of modifying any part of the system. For example: "Anyone who makes a change to the system without prior notification and approval, will be shot on sight."

Such policies are fundamentally inapplicable to today's *strategic applications networks*. First of all, it is unlikely that one organization controls an entire

145

strategic network: customers, suppliers, and users all contribute to the network, and the lines between "user" and "owner" have become increasingly blurred. Even if you could identify the user responsible for making a change to "your" network, if that user is a customer, you cannot shoot one of your customers! Yet, the network will *not* remain static as changing user requirements on each application will force changes in the network.

The Supernet™ Solution*

The *only* viable solution is for the network manager to develop or buy tools that can detect changes and modify the appropriate data translation routines in the SURROUND^{SM} environment. Because of the modular design of the SURROUND^{SM} system, swift modifications can be made to the "filters" that translate information between different systems. Because these filters are extremely compact, modifications can be made within minutes.

Another challenge is identifying which filter or filters need to be altered for a given application change, since a single application can require many

*For further discussion of the role of the CIO in network management, see John J. Donovan, "Beyond Chief Information Officer to Network Manager," *Harvard Business Review*, Sept. - Oct. 1988.

filters. To that end, it is possible to construct a "filter table" in the SURROUND^{SM} environment which automatically finds the filters affected by a particular change. In conventional environments, finding and fixing a translation program could take weeks, if it could be accomplished at all.

In the future, expert systems will be able to automatically detect, and in some cases even correct for, application changes. Test versions of such expert systems exist today, and are being incorporated into the SURROUND^{SM} environment.

Putting the right type of strategic network management into place is a crucial step in harnessing the potential benefits of strategic information technology. In fact, there is no last step — an organization must be committed to continually repeating and refining the process of strategic advantage.

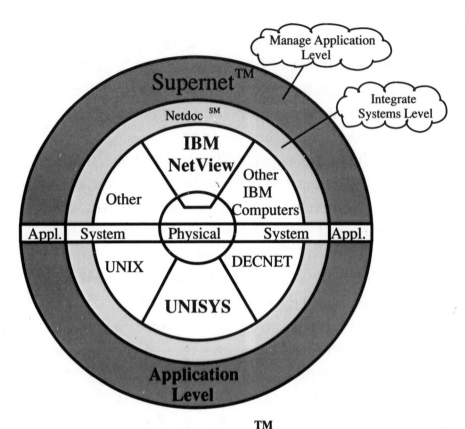

The Supernet[TM]
Network Management Architecture

FIRST STEPS:

1. Put into place the physical-level network management tools to service your physical network management needs.

148

2. Put into place the system-level network management packages to manage each one of your systems properly.

3. Integrate these systems to produce a comprehensive and consistent user interface to heterogeneous systems-level network management.

4. Put in place the tools to detect, and alert the network manager to, applications changes.

IX

SUMMARY

- The transition to strategic computing and communications will bring change to many parts of your organization.

- Change means gains but it also means losses. How do you handle losses?

- Change must be managed properly within your organization so that you can move quickly to implement and benefit from strategic applications.

Have you recently had projects delayed or even cancelled because of individuals' (or whole departments') resistance to change? What structures and policies are in place at your organization to help people deal with change in their working environment?

Managing Change

Change — and the management of change — is the top concern of senior executives today.
> Cambridge Technology Group
> Surveys of CEOs

You are change experts, but at this time there is a difference ... Now for the first time, I hear words like "survival," "maintenance," and "avoid stagnation" ... The kinds of changes have changed ... the organization's and individual's "ante is upped."
> David E. Morrison, M.D.
> Morrison Associates Ltd.

No company is safe ... There is no such thing as a "solid," or even substantial, lead over one's competitors. Too much is changing for anyone to be complacent. Moreover, the 'champ to chump' cycles are growing ever shorter...
> Tom Peters
> in *Thriving on Chaos*

Senior managers in every line of business are very concerned about **change**.* And for good reasons. The competitive world today is changing more rapidly than ever before and <u>organizations are forced to adapt quickly if they are to retain their competitive edge. "Adapting quickly" means dealing with constant change within the organization</u>. Change is necessary, therefore — but how can you manage change, and help your organization to adapt more smoothly?

Further, if you believe any of what we've discussed in Chapters 1-8, you will have to change something in your organization. How will you implement this change? That's what this chapter is about.

CHANGE HURTS

Do you have some old clothes in your closet that you have not worn for over a year? What would you do if your spouse (or friend) came in at this moment and proclaimed she or he had just given those clothes to the Salvation Army.... Even though you might never have worn those clothes again, the fact that they were in your closet meant a lot to you — and the

*Parts of this chapter are based on lectures by David Morrison, M.D., at the Cambridge Technology Group. For further information on Doctor Morrison's seminars, contact Morrison Associates Ltd., 650 First Bank Dr., Palatine, IL 60067

152

change of having them disappear is distinctly un-
pleasant.

Change hurts people because it inevitably involves a loss. Even a "positive" change, like a promotion, brings gains (salary increase, etc.) but also
losses (e.g. familiar office, altered relations with co-
workers, and perhaps a move to a new town and a
new house). Although you may initially focus on the
gains of a recent change, the losses — both real and
imagined — will eventually make themselves felt.

EXAMPLE OF CHANGE IN ROLE

For 20 years the CIO has been concerned with a
centralized operation of his data processing. The
"old days" of comfortable, centralized computer
systems are gone. We have talked at various times
about the forces driving the change toward decentralization in computing and communications. Let's
review them briefly:

Decentralization is happening because:

1. Strategic applications tend to be decentralized
   systems, tying together the systems in other
   organizations over which your CIO has no
   control.

2. The natural proclivity of users for ownership is bringing specialized computers into offices — they can even hide them in their stamp budgets!

3. With mergers and acquisitions, decentralized computing facilities are inevitable, as each acquisition may have their own systems.

4. Expert systems are developed most easily on small machines, and then require connections to data residing on other systems.

5. Software development productivity is higher on small machines for many applications, hence you will end up with a mixed environment.

6. Small, decentralized machines are for some applications a more economical way of distributing computing power to many users. (e.g. the cost per MIPS — Millions of Instructions Per Second — for an 80386-type machine is approximately $2000; the cost per MIPS of an IBM 3090 may be as high as $200,000.)

7. New processor technologies (e.g. parallel processors) may have to be integrated with existing systems.

There is no way to stop this from happening. The question is: how will these changes impact your organization and its staff, and how can you make it happen with a minimum of disruption? Let's look first at who gets affected, and how.

You may always have some portion of your data processing centralized, but it is inevitable that some component will be decentralized. Hence, the fundamental role of your CIO will change. Logically speaking, the CIO will become more strategic, more concerned with the network, and less concerned with the day–to–day operation of the computers. This is just one example of the type of change that you'll have to manage in your organization.*

TECHNOLOGICAL CHANGES — OPPORTUNITY OR CRISIS?

When steam–powered ships were first introduced, what was the reaction of the sailing industry? They refused to accept the technological change — they added larger sails and more masts. Hence, they lost a whole strategic advantage and opportunity.

*For further discussion of the changing role of the CIO, see John J. Donovan, "Beyond Chief Information Officer to Network Manager," *Harvard Business Review*, Sept. - Oct. 1988.

Changing information technology is now challenging organizations with similar opportunities or crises. Technological changes that you must take advantage of include the following: Tactical batch systems are changing to strategic on-line applications. Closed, centralized systems are yielding to a new world of connectivity and open architectures. Decision support functions are in some cases being replaced by expert systems that not only advise on, but actually **make** decisions. Traditional computers are being challenged by parallel processors (see Chapter 11) that provide 100 times more processing speed. Data processing is giving way to network management as the "top concern" of MIS departments. Single-vendor presence in your organization is giving way to multi-vendor architectures with the advent and acceptance of standards like UNIX. And after reading this book, traditional "pillage and burn" strategies are being supplemented by new approaches such as SURROUND.^{SM}

Are you going to get your organization to adapt to these technologies? Or are you going to settle for just making bigger sails and adding another mast?

ROLES OF INDIVIDUALS

Your CIO is changing to be more focused on what the technology can do rather than what the technology *is*. The CIO is going to be more concerned with the return on investment, profitability and customer satisfaction then with MIPS and CPU utilization.

Your users are changing to be the drivers of the technology and no longer the passive victims of the technological voodoo and jargon. The SUR-ROUND[SM] approach gives them the democratization of technology.

How are you going to implement these changes in your organization? They seem so logical; but remember your reaction when your favorite old pair of trousers that you hadn't worn in a year was thrown out.

YOUR GAME PLAN FOR CHANGE

Address and neutralize all your organization's impediments to change. Seven major impediments to change are listed below, along with actions you can take to overcome them.

1. Lack of Vision

You as a senior officer of your organization have a vision for your organization, sometimes referred to as "goals" or a "mission statement," and usually a vision for implementing those goals. How do you get everyone to change to see that vision?

· <u>Give them structure</u>. It was said for thousands of years before Darwin, people saw the bones in the rocks, but without the model and structure that Darwin gave us, they never saw them as bones.

· <u>Never miss an opportunity to present your vision</u>. Winston Churchill said, "Never, never give up." There will always be some analogy that may make people see what you mean.

With respect to the sorts of strategic applications we've been talking about here, live demonstrations can give people a structure and present opportunities for the advocates to explain their vision over and over again. Hence our advocacy of prototyping strategic applications.

2. Failure to Handle the Change Curve

When people are asked to undertake a project that involves changing attitudes and routines, their level of enthusiasm and confidence tends to go through a fairly predictable evolution. At the start of the project, enthusiasm is extremely high, and overwhelming success due to the new approach seems inevitable. But as soon as the project starts running into its first snags and setbacks, massive disillusion-ment often replaces the boundless confidence and failure suddenly looms large over the project. As the problems get worked out, the project team gradually rebuilds its enthusiasm to a more realistic level.

The danger in this roller coaster ride of emotions is that the project will suffer irreparable damage when people reach the stage where confidence plummets. There are two things project leaders can do to minimize the problem. <u>First, the leader can try to hold down the unrealistic expectations the team tends to develop in the first stage</u> by helping the team anticipate some of the problems they are likely to en-counter and understand any limitations of the new approach; if the first peak of enthusiasm isn't quite as high, then the team doesn't have as far to fall when reality starts to set in. Second, the team leader can try to <u>keep the team focused on its goals</u> when it reaches the spirit-sapping second stage, rather than letting the team wallow in discouraging details of tempo-rary problems. It's crucial at this stage to keep things as stable, routine and predictable as possible; people who are already on unfamiliar territory may be tempted to revert to older, more familiar approaches when faced with any additional changes or surprises.

It is important to realize in this context that managers are often "ahead" of their staff on the change curve, hitting peaks and valleys slightly before everyone else. Keep this in mind. Tell the staff about the curve and what to expect — openness is the best way to eliminate suspicion.

3. Defensiveness and Threats

Defensiveness impairs a person's ability to ever see the need for the change, much less act on it. New technologies are very threatening, especially something as radically new as SURROUND^{SM} technology, especially from people who are very entrenched in established "ways of doing things" and who feel threatened by the new technology. This threat posed by new technology will often include technical people, and almost always includes vendors of equipment and software. How do you thwart defensiveness so that people can react to change?

The solution is to <u>focus everyone on the goals of the organization</u>: to keep them from dwelling on their personal "fiefs" and fears. By keeping people goal-oriented and moving the application development process along quickly, defensiveness and threats can be minimized and — where they do occur — exposed as the non-productive behavior they are.

4. Impediment To Change — Bureaucracy

<u>Keep it moving</u>. Many organizations have estab-

160

lished lengthy and cumbersome processes to review and approve each stage of application development. That's acceptable when the application development process itself is lengthy and cumbersome as it traditionally has been, and when the application itself is tactical rather than strategic in nature. Such review processes are anathema to high-speed strategic application development. Subjecting a three-month project to a six-month review process will kill the project's momentum, dampen enthusiasm, and burden the process with unnecessary and even damaging changes. More importantly, it can result in missed strategic opportunities.

To avoid these problems, don't kill the entrepreneur. When a Xerox SWAT team realized that it was in danger of becoming bogged down in delays over approving a hardware vendor for the project at hand, the team won higher-level approval to circumvent corporate policy and simply continued on with the project without waiting for vendor selection.

5. Envy

Envy — the wish to destroy those who have "more" somehow — is a serious problem and can easily arise if SWAT team members, for example, are perceived as "different" from everyone else.

It's a good idea to channel overly competitive

feelings away from the job. A solution is to form user groups, in which many people who use or are impacted by new, existing or proposed systems meet on a regular basis to provide direct input to development teams. These groups will broaden the base of people in the organization who feel they are contributing to the new applications, and thus will act as change agents.

<u>You can also continually move people into the strategic applications process.</u> When a SWAT team has accomplished a highly visible and successful project and is about to start another, it's a good time to look into forming one or two more SWAT teams. A single SWAT team can be perceived as elitist, while multiple SWAT teams means that a larger number of people become directly involved with the new approaches—people who will feel ownership in the new approaches and who are likely to serve as change agents. In addition, multiple teams will mean that more strategic systems can be brought on line faster, resulting in even more rapid attainment of organizational goals.

6. Lack of Support Structure for Change

SWAT teams will do best in an environment that is designed to nourish creativity and innovation—an environment very different from that of the tradi-

162

tional systems development group. Organizations should consider setting aside facilities for these teams, along with funding to allow exploring new ideas and techniques in strategic application development. Some SWAT team members should be placed permanently in their new positions, establishing a solid core of expertise from which temporary SWAT team members can draw. Textron-Lycoming formed such a greenhouse, resulting in a stream of successful SURROUND^{SM} projects.

Building "infrastructure" within the organization is important, but getting senior executives on the side of the projects is especially critical. <u>Top management should be the first to see new demonstrations and project leaders should ensure that they can make their case in business terms that executives will appreciate</u>. Gaining support of the CEO is helpful, of course, but leaders should aim for a broad, critical mass of backers among top management rather than depending on the support of any one key manager. At a major U.S. bank, project advocates arranged for a major presentation of the new technologies and approaches to the Chairman and all the Vice-Chairmen of the Board—but it wasn't until the technical people "bought into" the project that they received support.

7. Crabs

"Crabs" are the people who prevent you from doing new things.

Remember that crabs can only move sideways or backward — never forward. Crabs will always try to pull back down those who climb toward the top of the basket. You can usually recognize them by the lack of constructive alternative proposals.

GET PEOPLE INVOLVED

There are many other change management tools that can be applied to dealing with issues arising with the transition to new approaches to strategic information technology. It is important that managers be sensitive to the fact that change is hard for everyone, and that people need to feel they have some control over change. Even the best ideas are doomed to failure if they are thrust upon people without regard for their need to make choices and participate in the formation of new routines. If these needs are taken into account, however, people's attitudes will reinforce rather than pull against the power of the new approaches. In the end, people—not technologies or methodologies—will determine the success of any efforts to make information play a more strategic role in the organization.

164

CRISIS IN TECHNOLOGY / 9

FIRST STEPS

1. Provide a structure and model for you staff of the vision you have for your organization. Focus on keeping everyone goal-oriented at all times, by insisting that all projects explicitly address their contribution to corporate goals, and by frequent demonstrations of goal-specific prototype projects. Goal orientation gives people a structure for grasping your corporate vision, keeps them from being defensive, and helps them through the inevitable change-curve slumps.

2. Encourage the formation of small user groups within your organization. This allows people to participate in decisions regarding the changes they will have to face, and increases their sense of control. It also reduces the potential for envy by giving everyone a chance to contribute. Finally, user groups provide a vehicle for redirecting competitiveness away from the job (and onto the athletic field, for instance).

3. Provide "greenhouse" facilities and funding for a SWAT team capability in your organization. The greenhouse environment allows you to "grow" additional SWAT teams over time, thus reducing their potentially elitist image and increasing their acceptance among your staff. The greenhouse also lets you circumvent lengthy review processes, hardware vendor selection procedures, and other institutional impediments that hinder the smooth flow of the new SWAT approach and highlight troublesome changes from established routines. SWAT team members should participate in frequent meetings/demos with top managers and with user groups, thereby spreading their newly gained vision upward and outward, acting as change agents, and keeping a wide range of staff "involved" in new developments.

4. Manage the change curve for all new projects, and train all managers to do the same. Managers should hold unrealistically high initial expectations at the outset of a new project, and should discuss the change curve with their staff to prepare them for what lies ahead.

5. Keep an eye out for crabs. If you recognize them early on, you may be able to change their attitudes before they cause great damage. If you cannot convince them to reform, crabs may have to be isolated or removed.

SUMMARY

· Three dramatic industrial changes have taken place in technology —

  ·standards, e.g. UNIX, ISDN, LANs, carriers are being accepted

  ·circuit costs are dropping

  ·true vendor competition is emerging

· You no longer need to be "locked" into a vendor for future applications because of proprietary operating systems or communications systems.

· You can reduce your computing and communications costs dramatically if you manage the vendor.

· You can increase the vendor focus on quality of service and responsiveness.

Here is how to dramatically increase the quality of your vendor service and reduce the cost of your computing and communications hardware — how you should operate with your vendor in this new era.

Seizing the New World — Vendor Competition

Through the 1980's, the cost of computing and communications dropped dramatically but only a fraction was passed on to the customer. But by 1988, a major change had begun — standards were being adopted allowing for <u>competition</u> — hence the customer gaining more and more control.

> Jack Scanlon
> Former V.P., AT&T
> Present COO, CTG

The trend toward standards and connectivity is a key factor in the growing popularity of distributed workstation environments; new technologies will continue to result in dramatic workstation performance enhancements.

> Andy Heller,
> V.P. and Fellow, IBM
> *Electronic Engineering Times*,
> March, 1988

How do you position your organization with the vendors in this new world?

THE DEMOCRATIZATION OF
INFORMATION COMPONENTS

Two key driving forces are dramatically shifting the buying behavior of strategic-thinking information managers.

1. The ever-accelerating advances in key technologies which continue to reduce the cost of information components; and
2. The broad move towards open standards specifying the interfaces to these information components.

The first force, accelerating technology, will permit the application of information components to the solution of key business problems where heretofore the cost-benefit was unattractive.

A simple example is the impact of the dramatic reduction in the price of a fax machine on how information is moved between companies. Over the last three years the price of a fax machine has declined by more than a factor of two. The result has been an increase in fax messages of 25% domestically and about twice that internationally. In business terms, there has been a reduction of fax costs compared to mail and especially express mail. At the same time, moving toward fax transmissions means orders of

171

magnitude improvements in responsiveness. A business needs to get the right information to survive; getting it before the competition means a competitive edge.

The second force, adoption of open standards, will permit many information component vendors to play and compete for market share, assuring that the cost reductions made possible by technological forces are effectively translated into price reductions. A simple example of the impact of the open standards force is the price of a UNIX computer compared to one based on a proprietary operating system such as DEC'sVMS™ or IBM's AS/400™. An approximate list price difference between these two choices is currently about 30%.

The reason is simple, good ole' COMPETITION. In the UNIX system case, more than 50 companies could respond to your request for a price while each of the alternatives would receive just one response. Basing your information systems needs on an open standards platform will give you freedom of choice and continuing price/performance improvements from the technology business. However, this new information democracy, like all democracies, will require a smart MIS electorate educated in the full scope of these choices in order to work well. Let's first probe more into whether the new technology and open standards are "real," and then explore how to vote smart with this new freedom of choice.

THE TECHNOLOGY FREIGHT TRAIN

Over what time frame would you agree with the statement "the price/performance of computing and communications has improved by 100:1." Thirty years? Twenty years? Ten years or perhaps for the pessimists — "I'm still waiting." The answer as illustrated below in Figure A is somewhat less than eight years — the last eight years.

Figure A
Technology Drivers Reducing Cost

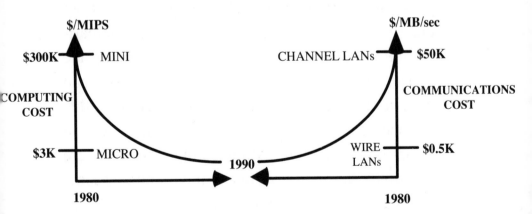

The left side of Figure A plots the improvement in the price/performance of computing beginning from 1980 up to 1988. The price/performance measurement is dollars/Millions of Instructions Per Second ($/MIPS). In 1980, a typical 32-bit multi-user mini would price out at about $300,000 and deliver about one MIPS, hence $300K/MIPS. In 1988, a 32-bit multi-user micro, such as an 80386-based computer multi-user system would price out at about $12,000 and deliver about 4 MIPS, yielding $3K/MIPS. The improvement in price/performance of computing during the last eight years is then 100:1.

One of the obvious benefits of this improvement in price/performance is that it has permitted the decentralization of computing, bringing the benefits of smaller growth increments and better local response to business applications. The purist will point out that this is not exactly an apples to apples comparison. For example, the 1980 mini had more upside expansion capability in the number of user ports and disk storage than a '386 micro. However, these differences are already small and, with advances in technology, are rapidly diminishing. The facts are that a user sitting in front of a terminal running some application on the 1980 mini and then the same ap-

174

plication on a 1988 micro, will observe price/performance improvement of about 100:1.

The right side of Figure A plots the improvements in the price/performance of local area computer communications. The price/performance measurement here is dollars/millions of bits per second ($/MB/sec). In 1980 the only practical Local Area Networks (LANs) were channel-based connections tying mainframe to mainframe. The more competitive offers delivered about 1 MB/sec and were priced around $50,000 per computer connection. In 1988, twisted pair or 'wire' LANs are available (adhering to an open standard such as IEEE 802.3), and providing at least 1 MB/sec for about $500 per connection. The improvement in price/performance is again, quite coincidentally, 100:1.

Again, the purist will point to some flaws in this comparison; but on the whole, it's accurate. One of the more obvious impacts of this improvement is that it's now cost-effective to interconnect PCs whereas eight years ago only a mainframe environment could bear this overhead.

What's fueling this technology freight train and what lies ahead? Fundamentally, it's the silicon integrated circuit technology, the microprocessor in particular. Today's micros are nearing the 10 MIPS

175

mark and RISC implementations assure 20-30 MIPS in just a few years at virtually no increase in price.

Moreover, the rate at which this technology is improving isn't flat — it's accelerating. Hence, while the 100:1 price/performance ratio was achieved in the last eight years, it is not outrageous to predict that it will be achieved again in the next four. These orders–of–magnitude improvements in technology have made PCs ubiquitous and will do the same for Fax machines. But how many businesses have revamped their operations to leverage this diffusion of sophisticated computing and communications across virtually their entire customer base? Very few. The reason is that business plans have traditionally assumed steady, incremental improvements, not 100:1 quantum jumps.

Ten years ago, would you have permitted the following business planning assumption to be used: "Computing and communications hardware costs will be zero."

At first glance, you would probably answer, "Certainly not." This is unfortunate, because relative to all of your other costs of operation (all of which have undoubtedly increased) this would have been absolutely the right assumption — dramatic enough to force you to completely rethink how these technologies could impact your operations. The good news is that you get another chance — the technology freight train presses on.

Yes, technology drives down cost and improves cost/performance curves. But why would a manufacturer pass these benefits on to the user in the form of reduced prices? Open standards leave no choice.

DON'T WORRY — BE OPEN!

The term "information component" was used early in this chapter. The information components of interest to a business and the emerging open standards affecting each one, are listed below:

Computers	UNIX
LANs	IEEE 802.3, 802.4, 802.5,
LAN Protocols	TCPIP/ISO/X.25
PBXs, Centrex	ISDN
T1 Circuit	De facto
800 Service	De facto

Note that *open* is a very important qualifier to 'standard.' It means there is a vendor-represented, but independent, body and evolving the standard so it both meets the market needs and permits many

177

players to compete. Some components, like T1, have become de facto standards due to ubiquity and publication of the interface specification, which permits others to design to them. But will these standards be adopted by the information vendors? Yes, because you, the customer, are insisting on the freedom of choice that standards permit.

Two examples of evidence of rapid migration by information vendors towards open standards are ISDN and UNIX. All digital switch vendors, both PBX and central office, are pitching ISDN capabilities on their emerging product lines. Similarly, a number of recent survey and market studies indicate that virtually every computer vendor of note is now offering (or planning to offer) a UNIX product line. Currently, a 22% market share for UNIX is forecast for "worldwide boxes shipped" by 1992.

Clearly, open standards are becoming a major force in the market. Competition under an open systems umbrella will insure that the price/performance cost benefits of the technology freight train are passed on to the customer. Information component vendors must move under this open standards umbrella to meet the new customer demand.

The combination of these two forces — an accelerating technology freight train and a movement toward open standards — will reduce the price of essential information components, improve the customer's ability to capitalize on the most recent technological advance, and greatly expand the number of information component vendors "running" for your business. If these trends are successfully exploited by your MIS department, then the continuing dramatic improvements in price/performance of technology can be used to reduce operating costs and problems in areas like order processing, inventory control, and billing. How must MIS departments adjust in order to marshal these new forces? It's definitely not going to be "business as usual."

FREEDOM OF CHOICE AND HOW TO USE YOUR VOTE

Your selecting an open systems information platform brings both enormous benefits to your organization and requires major changes in how your staff operates. Earlier chapters have explored the technical changes which an open system platform requires. Thinking "SURROUND^{SM} architecture" rather than "pillage and burn" at the systems level and basing implementations on portable software technology to permit both vendor choice and technology insulation are examples of much change. Now it's time to

179

<u>discuss another, and just as important transformation which must be made — dealing with information vendors in this new era.</u>

YOUR OLD WAY

Due primarily to lack of choice, the purchasing decision-making process for information components for most large companies has, for the most part, looked like this:

Figure B
Traditional Purchase Decision-making Process

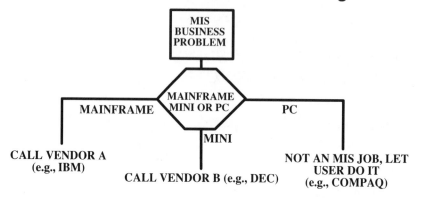

The first place where real 'choice' crept into this process was at the PC level as DOS clones arrived. Only recently have PC choices been pulled back toward a centralized decision making process. This happened because of a growing need to interconnect PCs with the rest of the corporate computing structure — primarily to improve access to corporate data.

NOW

More recently, real choice has crept into the mini computer area via UNIX, and in the LANs and WANs (Wide Area Networks) that connect the mini server to the PC below it and the mainframe above it. While some non-clone choice is appearing at the mainframe level, again via UNIX, it is unlikely that this will have a major impact on most businesses due to the extensive investment in record formats at the mainframe (these would have to be changed to migrate to UNIX). The SURROUND^{SM} architecture resolves this issue more elegantly, relegating the mainframe to a giant file server while permitting the migration of computing to distributed, more cost-effective minis and PCs which *are* based on standards.

181

Hence, in a few short years the MIS decision makers went from a few or no choices to many, and it's just beginning. The complexity of these choices is increasing geometrically — choices at each level of computing and the communications links in between compounded by an ever-increasing number of vendors capitalizing on open standards to offer products. How can the MIS decision makers interact effectively in this milieu? Surprise, surprise — learn from the Feds.

REQUEST IT/PROVE IT/PRICE IT

For reasons totally independent of the move to open standards, the Feds learned a long time ago how to force information vendors to give them choice — albeit initially miniscule. It's the 'RFI/RFQ/RFP Show me, then buy' process by which most federal information procurements are now made. In the early days, 'functional spec' was the only umbrella under which a choice could be made. Under this system, a spec which requested a low-flying bird detector system for Capitol Hill sidewalks could be responded to with computer control systems written in Esperanto, as long as the functional specs were met.

The government quickly learned that meeting

functional specs wasn't enough. In the case outlined above, for example, the training cost to the government for Esperanto programming would turn out to be a major cost factor and a contributor to technological obsolescence. Spurred on by these hard lessons, it was the government, and not private industry, which launched and frequently paid for the development of key standards.

As a consequence, government RFPs are now frequently bounded by specific standard requirements, which improve the government's ability to leverage the best price from the vendors and avoid technological obsolescence. The most recent case was the procurement of new Air Force computer systems, which specified UNIX System V. Note also that simply responding to a bid, meeting the specs, and adhering to the standards isn't good enough. Live test demos are frequently required where the vendors must demonstrate their capability against specific criteria — this is the 'show me' step. <u>Vendors who survive up to this point then compete for the business on price, reputation, service and responsiveness to you!</u>

Due to the plethora of government regulations, this process takes years to complete and as such is not acceptable to the commercial customer. However, a streamlined version of this 'request it/prove it/price it' scenario is already being adopted by many large businesses and is a must if the benefits of open standards are to be realized by MIS decision makers.

FIRST STEPS:

· In summary, technology will continue to drive the cost from information components at an ever-accelerating rate.

· However, for you the customer to take advantage of this, your solutions must be based on open computing and communications systems which will insure that the technology benefits are passed on to the end user.

· The buying process for the technology decision makers must shift from 'pick a vendor' to 'put out a request for a bid' to 'permit the forces of competition to bring the best value to the table.'

· Finally, paper responses aren't enough. A 'prove it' stage is required to insure that both functionality and performance are being delivered.

XI

SUMMARY

· New and emerging technologies represent opportunities that can make your organization's information more effective.

· Expert systems allow you to capture the experience of your best staff, and leverage their knowledge throughout the organization.

· Parallel processor computers are cost-effective, high-speed machines that can give you a competitive edge in time-critical, data-intensive applications.

· User interface technologies give you ways of expanding your user base and of promoting the effective use of your information resources.

· All of these technologies can be integrated smoothly and economically with your existing systems by means of the SURROUND^{SM} technology.

Have you ever resisted the introduction of a new technology into your organization because it was incompatible with your existing installations? Has this affected your competitive position?

XI

The Future — Weapons You Must Consider

Who's lined up at the door [of MIT's Media Lab]? The business studs... Their interest is simple: they want to stay in business, and if ...the business environment shifts, they have got to shift with it, preferably just ahead of it.

> Stewart Brand
> in *The Media Lab:*
> *Inventing the Future at MIT*

Your business can create its own expert systems, and doing so may save you substantial sums of money ... [the number of expert systems] being used on a day–to–day basis ... skyrocketed to 1,400 in 1988 [from 50 in 1987].

> *Boston Globe*
> 27 September 1988

The problem is getting the small new machines [with expert systems] to fit into the world of the big old ones [with the necessary data].

> *Fortune Magazine*
> 12 October 1987

188

We'll take a look at three technologies you must consider for your arsenal of weapons: expert systems, parallel processor computers, and user interface technologies. These technologies are here today, and explosive developments will make them even more powerful in the near future. These technologies have the potential to produce order–of–magnitude improvements in the power and accessibility of your information systems. If a new technology is strategic to your organization's goals, you can't afford to ignore it for long. How can you identify the important technologies for your organization, and how can you take advantage of them? <u>Once again, the SURROUND^{SM} architecture is the key</u>.

EXPERT SYSTEMS

Expert systems attempt to capture and duplicate a specific part of human thought: the process of *judgment*. Usually, it's the judgment of one or more experts that you want to duplicate — hence the term "expert system." Why haven't expert systems been commonly used in the past?

There are three pitfalls that can make the implementation of expert systems a difficult process. First, <u>expert systems only work well in certain areas;</u> they cannot be applied to every task of an organization. Second, within the correct areas, some <u>technical considerations must be met to make the expert system feasible and worthwhile</u>. Finally, technology must be on hand to <u>allow the expert system to extract necessary data from existing computer systems</u>. Let's look at each of these issues in turn.

AUTOMATING THE JUDGMENT CALLS OF THE EXPERT

Expert systems work in areas where judgment calls are important to your business activities. One illustration of this might be the difference between the "best" and "worst" salespeople in a telemarketing organization. Some salespeople will sell substantially more than others even though they are of equal intelligence and are selling the same products. Why?

By questioning and observing the better salespeople, it is possible to formulate a set of rules that they seem to follow, and when these rules are given to the less successful salespeople, their performance improves dramatically. <u>This sort of encapturing, and the subsequent automation, of systematic rules is the essence of expert systems</u>.

A simple financial decision support tool utilizing expert system technology might take information about an individual as input (earnings, marital status, etc.) and apply a set of rules to this input to recommend a mix of savings accounts, checking accounts, treasury bills, etc. (A typical rule might look something like this: "if the client is single and has a fixed income and a high risk profile, then recommend investment portfolio X.")

In another example, a major food company built a commodity buyer's workstation that includes an expert system which recommends buy and sell options on the basis of market and other indicators. And a major bank recently built a telemarketing workstation that incorporates an expert system that recommends cross-selling approaches based on customer and account information.

Expert systems work best in areas where you would like to <u>leverage an expert's judgment and experience over a wider range of people</u>. Once you've identified such an area, it's time to look at technical feasibility and a "business case."

WILL IT WORK?

A short checklist lets you quickly evaluate the <u>technical feasibility</u> of a proposed expert system. If you can answer all five of these questions with "yes," then the planned expert system application can be built:

191

1. Can you <u>identify experts</u> who are significantly "better than average" at this job?

2. Is there a <u>specialized body of knowledge</u> and experience that enables the experts to do their job well?

3. Is this <u>knowledge at the right stage</u> of development? (It should be somewhere between an exact science and a "black art.")

4. Are the <u>experts capable of articulating their knowledge</u>? (It may require a lengthy interview process.)

5. Does the knowledge involve <u>chains of reasoning</u> (a sequential process of intermediate "decisions" that eventually lead to a recommendation)?

After establishing technical feasibility, take a look at the business case by estimating the cost and the payoff of the proposed system. Cost varies with the complexity of the system, which is usually measured in the number of decision rules the system employs. Up to about 400 rules (a moderately complex system of that size can already be very useful), the cost curve is fairly flat, and such a system might cost between $50,000 and $100,000. For more complex systems, costs rise much more steeply.

The payoff may be quickly calibrated by estimating the value of half the difference in performance between your experts and an "amateur." This is a good estimate of what the expert system will give you in improved decision-making performance.

THE CRITICAL ELEMENT: INFORMATION

To make good decisions, you need good judgment and good information. An expert system embodies the best judgment of your staff, but without access to the best information, the system will be stymied. Chances are, this information already exists somewhere on the computers within your organization, or on public information services, as it does in the examples above. What you need is a quick link between this information and the expert system — and that is where the SURROUND[SM] technology comes in.

Whether the expert system requires market trend data for market strategy suggestions, or customer account information for cross-sell recommendations, SURROUND[SM] technology can provide a rapidly im-

193

plemented, reliable, and flexible way of getting the
data from existing systems into the new expert system application. There is no need for expensive
modifications to your existing systems, and no need
to change the expert system every time you want to
feed in data from an additional source. Within the
SURROUND^{SM} "envelope," the new expert system
becomes just one more application that can be integrated with your other information systems in a strategic network.

PARALLEL PROCESSOR COMPUTERS

Parallel processor computers can give you tremendous computing power for applications where
speed is critical. There are parallel processor computers on the market today that are two orders of
magnitude faster than the best traditional machines.
That's like flying from New York to L.A. in three
minutes instead of six hours!

Not only do parallel processor computers work
faster than traditional machines — they also provide
computing power more economically. Instead of
doing all the work on one expensive processor, they
divide the job between a large number of simpler,
linked processors that work simultaneously ("in parallel").

As with expert systems, the difficulty with parallel processor computers lies in finding the correct applications and then integrating the new hardware into your existing systems architecture. What exactly can parallel processing do for you, and how can you fit this technology into your information systems strategy?

WHEN SPEED/CAPACITY COUNTS

Must you wait for a faster Cray machine (once every five years) to take advantage of high-speed processing? Not necessarily. Processing speed — how quickly the computer can digest information — depends on whether a task can be broken down into more than one parallel subtask. For example, if you wanted to search 4,000 libraries for all documents relating to oil prices, you could assign a serial computer to search for each document in sequence. But with a parallel processor, you could assign 4,000 *processors* to search each library <u>simultaneously</u>, reducing search time by a factor of 4,000!

<u>This parallel processing capability is here *now*</u>. It is a revolution that gives the effect of a 6,000 MIP machine today for <u>certain</u> applications — especially those types of business applications in which you need more computer <u>capacity</u>.

195

Usually these applications involve the processing of large volumes of data in a short period of time. Examples might include a system that manages a delicate manufacturing process in "real-time" (while it is happening), a system that simulates a complex biological process for doctors during an operation, an application that analyzes moving video images in real-time, or a system that involves a high-speed text search through whole libraries of information. For "emergency management" and real-time decision support applications, processing speed can be the single most critical factor.

When you are faced with a time-critical, data-intensive application that is just not running fast enough, your first reaction might be to go with a faster computer. Using traditional machines, this can get expensive or impossible.

Parallel processor machines offer high speed using conventional technology. Because they make use of conventional chips, and get their speed by using a large number of identical processors, their cost only goes up in direct proportion to speed. And, by adding more processors, it is possible to get a parallel processor computer customized for just about any speed you want.

Parallel processor computers are available today

from a variety of vendors, and represent a proven technology that continues to evolve rapidly.

PARALLEL PROCESSORS AND YOUR EXISTING ENVIRONMENT

A parallel processor machine gives you unprecedented computing power and lets you speed up critical processes. But how can you integrate this new piece of equipment into your existing systems?

To maximize its usefulness, the parallel processor computer will have to receive information from, and return results to, the other applications on your information systems. Moving all of your applications to parallel processors is unrealistic. What you need is a technology that lets you link the parallel processor machine and its time-critical applications to your existing applications with minimal effort and disruption.

SURROUND^{SM} is this technology. Using the SURROUND^{SM} approach, you can integrate the parallel processor computer into your existing systems, drawing the necessary data from your present applications and placing only the truly time-critical functions on the new machine. Like the expert system, the parallel processor becomes one more part of your strategic network.

197

UNIX also has an important part to play in these systems for two reasons — portability and environment. <u>If speed is truly critical to your competitive success, you will need to replace your machines frequently to stay on the forefront of evolving technology</u>. Rewriting your applications each time you replace the underlying hardware is expensive and time-consuming. By using the UNIX operating system on these machines, you can minimize the work involved in <u>porting</u> to better machines later. The <u>environment</u> of UNIX is such that UNIX itself automatically breaks up a job into many pieces allowing all the subworkers (the many CPUs) to execute each one simultaneously.

USER INTERFACE TECHNOLOGIES

Can the people you want to use the technology use the technology? Or is your user interface too "techie," technically oriented? <u>The key to such increased usability of your system, and in the effectiveness of the human-computer interaction, is the user interface.</u>

CURRENT USER INTERFACE TECHNOLOGY IS PRIMITIVE

Consider talking to a person that makes no facial expressions or makes no utterances of agreement or disagreement. What's wrong? It's a one-way com-

munication. A computer gives little positive rein-
forcement during its interaction — it doesn't grunt, it
doesn't talk, it doesn't nod its terminal.

Consider arriving home and your spouse (or
friend) asking you, "Did you buy it?" You know exactly what he/she means. Ask that same question of
your computer. It knows nothing about you. And as
the years go on, it never learns.

Consider your spouse talking to you. As you
leave the room, he or she speaks louder. And when
you're out of sight, he or she stops talking (usually!).
Consider your terminal spewing out data. What does
it do when you leave the room?

In short, that interface between the human and the
computer is awful. If a fellow human being treated
you that way, you would no longer interact with him
or her. And yet tradition has trained us into thinking
that with computers only the most primitive interac-
tions are possible.

ALL IS CHANGING

Voice recognition, touch screens, two-way
video, and image processing are all now available.
And if you use SURROUND^{SM} architecture, you do not
need to throw away your current systems to incorporate these new interfaces.

199

FIRST STEPS:

1. List the instances in your line of business where expert judgment is of paramount importance. Where would more informed, uniform decision-making be of the greatest value? Have someone answer the five feasibility questions for each application and do a cost-benefit analysis for each.

2. Identify instances in your business where speed is critical. Is the processing power of your computers a bottleneck anywhere? Get access to a parallel processor and start experimenting.

3. Assign someone in your organization to investigate the currently available voice, touch, video user interface hardware. Purchase one of these interfaces and integrate with your current systems using SURROUND^{SM} architecture.

XII

Conclusion

Congratulations! You are now prepared to apply these concepts and methodologies we have discussed to realize and improve your organization's strategic advantage.

Using the CAMBRIDGE METHOD℠ discussed in this book, you and your business executives can get what you want, and get it <u>now</u>. The democratization of technology is placing this capability in the hands of the people who most need it.

The approach described in *Crisis in Technology* frees your organization from being held hostage by your competitive forces and by your own technologies. The solution of SWAT prepares you for the present and future onslaught of new technologies, which could be a crisis if your competitor uses them, but which will be an opportunity if you use them first. With the CAMBRIDGE METHOD℠, <u>you can!</u>

FIRST STEPS

1. Identify a strategic application.

2. Form a SWAT team.

3. Develop a business case.

4. Pick a neutral environment suitable for both users and technologists to implement your first application using <u>the</u> SWAT <u>solution</u>.

5. Manage the change and continue to add value to your strategic applications.

6. Do it NOW — don't let the crabs get you.

Thank you.

Additional Readings

Allison, *Essence of Decision*, (Little Brown)

Brand, *The Media Lab: Inventing the Future at MIT* (Viking)

Cohen, *You Can Negotiate Anything* (Citadel Press)

Davis and Lenat, *Knowledge–Based Systems in Artificial Intelligence* (McGraw–Hill)

Donovan, "Beyond Chief Information Officer to Network Manager," *Harvard Business Review*, Harvard University, Cambridge, MA

Johnson & Sirbu, *Telecommunications Alternatives* (Rand)

Kernighan and Ritchie, *'C' Programming Language* (Prentice–Hall)

Kernighan and Pike, *The UNIX Programming Environment* Prentice–Hall)

Levitt, *The Marketing Imagination* (MacMillan)

MacFarlan and McKenney, *Corporate Information Systems Management* (Richard D. Irwin, Inc.)

Madnick & Donovan, *Operating Systems* (McGraw–Hill)

Nolan, *Managing the Data Resource Function* (West Publishing Company)

Peters, *Thriving on Chaos* (Knopf)

/ ADDITIONAL READINGS

Porter, *Competitive Advantage* (MacMillan)

Rockart & DeLong, *Executive Support Systems* (Dow Jones–Irwin)

Vaillant, *Adaptation to Life* (Little, Brown & Co.)

Index